REMEMBERING

ALBANY

REMEMBERING

ALBANY

Heritage on the Hudson

DON RITTNER

Charleston   London

THE
History
PRESS

A view up State Street from the Knickerbocker Press Building. The capitol can be seen at top, along with the new State Education Building, which was being built in this 1911 photograph. The Lyon block is on the left and the Cathedral of Immaculate Conception is also to the top left. *Courtesy of the Library of Congress.*

Published by The History Press
Charleston, SC 29403
www.historypress.net

First published 2009

Manufactured in the United States

ISBN 978.1.59629.770.8

Library of Congress Cataloging-in-Publication Data

Rittner, Don.
Remembering Albany : heritage on the Hudson / Don Rittner.
p. cm.
ISBN 978-1-59629-770-8
1. Albany (N.Y.)--History. 2. Albany (N.Y.)--Social life and customs. I. Title.
F129.A357R58 2009
974.7'43--dc22
2009021536

To Jennifer and Jason, Christopher, Kevin and Jackson

Contents

CONTENTS

Acknowledgements

M any people have graciously provided photographs or information for this book. I would like to thank Mike Engle, Efner Research Library, Tom Clement, Library of Congress (HABS), Lisa Lewis and John Wolcott. Special thanks go to Ellen Gamache from the Albany Public Library and Chris Hunter, archivist with the Schenectady Museum Archives, for allowing the use of their excellent collections. Special thanks go to my editor Kate Pluhar at The History Press.

Introduction

Albany, New York, was explored by Henry Hudson in 1609, but it took a handful of Dutch explorers to settle the region with a small trading fort in 1614. Since then, the city has been making a mark on history for nearly four hundred years.

Albany is located about 150 miles north of New York City on the western banks of the Hudson River, or as the original inhabitants, the Mohicans, called it, *Muhhekunnetuk*—"the river that flows both ways."

The Albany fur trade is long gone, but the city has transformed itself into one that specializes in education and politics. There are a dozen colleges and universities in the area, and Albany has always had politics running through its veins. It was here that the struggle between the Dutch and English came to a head in 1664. It was in Albany that Benjamin Franklin delivered his Plan of Union in 1754, and the city became the capital of the state in 1797. Today more than 25 percent of the population works in government-related jobs.

This collection of articles written over a period of several years covers a wide variety of subject areas on Albany's interesting history, from the RCA dog Nipper that towers over the landscape to the invention of perforated toilet paper. Being nearly four centuries old can make you a bit eccentric, and Albany has had its share of interesting events and notable citizens. The more than thirty stories in this book will give you a sizable sample.

PART I

Oddities

A Yankee Doodle Mystery

There is a large two-story brick building in the city of Rensselaer, facing the west near the Hudson River that is owned by the State of New York. Known as Fort Crailo, there has been more mystery surrounding this site than a children's *Goosebumps* story.

It has been reported that the song "Yankee Doodle" was written here sometime in the 1750s by Dr. Richard Schuckburg while sitting on a well in the rear of the fort. Schuckburg was an army surgeon during the French and Indian War, and supposedly he wrote the song as a derisive tune mocking the colonials, some of whom dressed in furs and buckskins. Apparently, he didn't take too well to the fact that they were not dressed spit and polish like the British troops.

Today, there are close to two hundred versions of "Yankee Doodle." Early versions were published on two American broadsides between 1775 and 1776, titled *The Farmer and his Son's Return from a Visit to the Camp* and *The Yankeys Return from Camp*. On both, the songs are identical.

In 1775, sheet music of "Yankee Doodle" appeared in London after news spread of the battle at Lexington, and the song was a big hit throughout England.

Fort Crailo as it appears today in Rensselaer. *Photo by Don Rittner.*

According to Thomas Anburey, a British soldier in 1777, "Yankee" is a term that is derived from the Cherokee word *eankke*, and it was used to mean "coward" or "slave." "Yankee" was used as an epithet for New Englanders by the Virginians because they didn't help them during a war with the Cherokees. Some historians have said that "Doodle" may mean fool or simpleton.

Despite the fact that "Yankee Doodle" began as ridicule, the colonials took the song and adopted it for their own. Thomas Anburey recorded that the colonials played "Yankee Doodle" when the British surrendered at Saratoga. It is also said that Cornwallis surrendered at Yorktown while the British played "The World Turned Upside Down" and the Americans played "Yankee Doodle."

The fort itself is not without mystery. During the early part of the twentieth century, the building was owned by a descendant of the Van Rensselaers. Mrs. Alan H. Strong sold it to the Daughters of the American Revolution in 1915. The State of New York eventually acquired it but decided it didn't like the looks of the building and "doodled" with it.

A comparison of early photos with those from the present reveals quite a change. Originally having a gambrel roof, it was removed and replaced with the present spout gabled roof. There was an entrance from the basement to the well that has been sealed off. Dormer windows were removed, and casement windows were put in with small diamond-shaped panes. Dutch half doors were added, Dutch fleur-de-lis wall ties were removed and other alterations were made over the objections of then state archivist Arnold Van Laer.

An addition to the main building was added about 1740. It has been said that a stone or brick with the letters "IVR" and the date "1740" exists on the east side of the northern door but is not visible today.

Part of the confusion about the construction of the building is due to the fact that no one, including Van Laer, could find a date of construction that would stick. Was it a Dutch house or colonial mansion?

Dates as early as 1642 were attributed to the building. This date, with the letters KVR, is inscribed on a stone in the basement foundation, along with another stone marked with the word "APOLENSIS," forming the last part of the name "Megapolensis." In 1661, there was mention of a farm called Crailo, which may have been an old farm of Evert Pels on the east side of the river that was taken over by Jeremias Van Rensselaer. Fort Crailo appears in 1663 in connection with the digging of the well.

The other mystery name is Do. or Dominie Megapolensis, who was hired by Van Rensselaer to minister for six years. The congregation built him a house but he didn't like it. So is this stone from the house he didn't use? How did it get in the foundation wall and why is the left part of the name covered with the north wall? Or, as another version has said, was the left part of the name simply broken off after the brick was recovered from his original house that was demolished?

There is also evidence that a fort was built in Greenbush to protect against Indian attack. In 1663, a new fort was built at the time of the massacre by the natives of Kingston settlers farther south. Since Fort Orange was in terrible shape, settlers fled to the fort called "cralo" erected on the patroon's farm at Greenbush. But this was also described as a little fort or fortification, not a two-story brick mansion.

The truth is out there, and it should become the noble quest of inspiring historians and archaeologists to discover the true history of Fort Crailo. In addition, Dr. Schuckburg died and was buried in Schenectady, but no one knows where.

A Tale of a Whale

For the length of most of the Hudson River to the base of the dam in Troy, the water is salty. It is technically not a river, but rather an estuary or fjord, a large, finger-like extension of the Atlantic Ocean. The Mohicans called it *Muhhekunnetuk*, meaning "the river that flows both ways." It's why we have tides in Albany and, occasionally, a rare sea visitor.

An old memorandum book of Antony de Hooges, secretary of the patroonship of Rensselaerswijck, describes a whale of a tale. Tucked among the mundane business records is reference to two sightings of "whales" in Albany in 1647. This book can be found in the New York State Archives and, translated, states:

Albany view in 1684. The Dutch Church and Fort Frederick can be seen. *Courtesy of John Wolcott.*

On the 29th of March in the year 1647 a certain fish appeared before us here in the colony, which we estimated to be of a considerable size. He came from below and swam past us a certain distance up to the sand bars and came back towards evening, going down past us again. He was snow-white, without fins, round of body, and blew water up out of his head, just like whales or tunas. It seemed very strange to us because there are many sand bars between us and Manhattan, and also because it was snow-white, such as no one among us has ever seen; especially, I say, because it covered a distance of 20 [Dutch] *miles of fresh water in contrast to salt water, which is its element. Only God knows what it means. But it is certain, that I and most all of the inhabitants* [watched] *it with great amazement. On the same evening that this fish appeared before us, we had the first thunder and lightening of the year.*

On the 19th of April in the year 1647 another fish appeared here around noon before Fort Orange with the high water (seafaring men who have sailed to Greenland judged it to be a whale). It was of considerable size as the previous one (we estimated it to be over 40 feet long). It was brown in color like a [word unknown] *with large fins on its back and blew water out of its head like the one before. He swam upstream against this extraordinary current. It seemed strange to me because it has been several years since a tuna has appeared here. It caused great amazement how the fish had swum so far and* [word unknown] *in this spring two such large fish should appear,* [word unknown] *is unheard of, for reasons stated about the previous fish.*

At forty feet long, the first visitor certainly may have been a whale. A white whale would have been a rare treat, perhaps an albino, but this first sighting could have been a dolphin or porpoise (all considered "whales"). They also have blowholes on top of their bodies. However, dolphins and porpoises have a dorsal fin that would have been obvious to the Dutch viewers. Whales, dolphins and porpoises all belong to the taxonomic order Cetacea. They are warm-blooded mammals that live in water, have hair on their bodies and nourish their young with milk, just like humans.

Heritage on the Hudson

There is a white whale (*Delphinapterus leucas*), the Beluga whale, which grows to about fifteen feet, but it lives in the Arctic and subarctic waters. It has been found in the St. Lawrence River in Canada and the Yukon in Alaska, so it was probably not the Albany visitor, unless it took a really wrong turn. Belugas are called sea canaries because they are very vocal with chirps, squeaks and clicks; the sighting mentioned no vocalization.

Since there are many early accounts of whales in early New York City (New Amsterdam) waters, it's not too much of a gamble to say that both of those sightings were in fact whales.

Additionally, in March 1647, Dutch traveler Adrian Van der Donk wrote that two whales of "common size" swam up the Hudson, one continuing all the way to the Cohoes Falls, and became stranded on an island (renamed Whale Island, now submerged). The residents of the Troy area boiled out the oil and left the carcass stinking up the area for weeks. Benjamin Hall, a lawyer who constructed the Hall Building (now Rice Building), wrote a humorous poem about it in 1866. Hall whimsically throws in the names of those contemporary Dutch residents who may have been there to see it all happen:

> *So the animal swam 'gainst the wind and the tide,*
> *Caring not if the river were narrow or wide,*
> *Rushing on like the tempest, and marking his path*
> *With the terrible waves of his foam-breathing wrath.*
>
> *But soon 'mid the islands off Rensselaerswyck's shore*
> *The animal floundered and snorted and tore;*
> *Stuck fast in the quicksand, unable to go,*
> *He blew out his life in a chorus of woe.*
>
> *As the spring floods subsided, the yeomanry came,*
> *To see the great monster without any name;*
> *Among them a skipper, renowned on the sea*
> *With a knowledge of fishes like Barnum, P.T.*
> *This skipper climbed up on the animal's back,*
> *Then wandered about with a varying tack,*

Pulled away at his flippers, examined his tail,
And said to the Dutchmen, "This here is a whale."

The people all came, with hatchets and saws,
And axes and cleavers, and meat-hooks and claws,
Determined to turn to their own private use
What before they had thought was a public abuse,
Prepared in great kettles his blubber to broil,
And try the great whale into barrels of oil.

The Skipper Jan Symensen ruled in the roast,
With Borssum and Stogpens and burgher Van Voorst.
Then Dirck Cornelissen came in for his share,
As did Jansen and Claessen,—which surely was fair.
Govert Loockmans was there with the Criegers and Pieters,
And Volckertsen, Symon Pos, Teunissen Meters;
Jan Tyssen, the trumpeter famed for his blowing,
And Wolfert Gerrittsen, a master at mowing;
Rutger Hendricksen, ale maker equal to Taylor;
Cornelis Tomassen, both blacksmith and nailer;
Carstenssen, the millwright, Laurenssen, the sawyer,
And Adriaen Van der Donck, sheriff and lawyer;
Jansen Stol, who at Beverwyck managed the ferry;
Pieter Bronck, at whose tavern so many got merry;
Gerrittsen van Bergen, the owner of acres;
The sportsman renowned, named Harry de Backers,
Of whom it is told that one day out of fun
He killed eleven gray geese at a shot from his gun;
Pels Steltyn, the brewer, and Jacob Wolfertsen;
Cornelis Crynnesen, Cornelis Lambertsen;
Claes Jansen van Waalwyck, Claes Jansen Yan Ruth,
And Megapolensis, a preacher of truth,

Sander Leendertsen Glen, a skilled Indian peddler,
And Mynderst der Bogart, a quarrelsome meddler.

Heritage on the Hudson

Antonie de Hooges, who to Anthony's Nose
Gave his name on the Hudson, and Andries de Vos;
Jan Labbadie, carpenter, native of France,
Who at Fort Orange led many a dance;
Gysbertsen, the wheelwright, who frequently spoke;
Jansen Dam, who in Council delighted to smoke;
Burger Joris, whose smithy stood under a tree;
Adriaensen van Veere, a freebooter free,
And Pieterse Koyemans, called Barent the miller,
Whose name in the manor was ever a pillar.

It would lengthen too much this unerring detail
To tell how by piecemeal they cut up the whale;
How the doughty old knights of the broad-sword appeared
When they brought down their blades as if nothing they feared;
How the butchers with cleavers dealt terrible blows,
And the children all scattered for fear of their toes;

At the end of a month from the time they began,
The oil ceased to flow, which so freely had ran.
Of the whale naught remained but his carcass and spine,
On which crows came to breakfast and oft stayed to dine.
An account which was kept showed the end of this toil
To be seventy-nine barrels five pipkins of oil.
Thus light was increased, and spread through the land,
Springing forth from the whale lying dead on the strand.

Ironically, Whale Island was not too far from the home of a young man who wrote two books out of his room facing the Hudson in Lansingburgh. Herman Melville would later write the classic whale story *Moby Dick* in 1851, 204 years after that whale beached not far from his home.

French Unjustly Fried?

Never let it be said that a congressman won't go out of his way to look idiotic. Just ask Representative Bob Ney, R-Ohio, the chairman of the Committee on House Administration, and his colleague Walter Jones, R-North Carolina. During the beginning of the Iraq war, Jones circulated a letter suggesting that the congressional cafeteria menus in the three House office buildings be changed, making "French fries" into "Freedom fries" and "French toast" into "Freedom toast." This was in retaliation over France's refusal to support the U.S. position on Iraq. Ney, who pushed it through, is quoted in the paper as saying, "This action today is a small, but symbolic effort to show the strong displeasure of many on Capitol Hill with the actions of our so-called ally, France." Well, as they say in France, "*Quels cretins.*"

These two boys have egg on their faces! If they knew a little history, they wouldn't be the current "toast" of the town for comedians and historians around the world.

First of all, French toast is not a "French" invention. Even funnier is that French toast is an American creation—more specifically, it has an Albany, New York birthright. You see, Joseph French, an Albany area tavern keeper in 1724, served his "French" bread for breakfast, but his poor knowledge of grammar prevented him from putting the possessive apostrophe after his name to read on his menu, correctly, "French's Bread."

In fact, the French call it "*pain perdu,*" which means "lost bread"; it's made from one- or two-day-old bread and is served mostly as dessert, not breakfast.

Now there was a recipe for "French Toasts" in 1660 that called for "French bread sliced and toasted, then soaked in wine, sugar and orange juice." Obviously, this is not even close to our traditional treat! I am now demanding that "French toast" officially be changed to "Albany toast," and instruct all local restaurants to make those changes in their menus.

On the other hand, France does claim the origin of French fries ("frites"), but also does nearby Belgium, which has more Belgian fry stands (*frietkots*) than breweries—and we all know how much the Belgians love their beer. In fact, many of the *frietkot* owners do so well that they drive around in Mercedes. To say that Belgians love Belgian *frieten* is an understatement. Perhaps the confusion began as early as the 1700s, when Thomas Jefferson served as ambassador to France. After enjoying the Belgian special (southern Belgium is also French speaking), he served them at Monticello to his guests as "Potatoes, fried in the French Manner." After all, he wasn't the ambassador of Belgium (which didn't even exist as a country until 1830), but of France, so the confusion is forgivable.

While both the French and Belgians claim the origin of the fry, it is known that by the 1830s both countries loved them. Today Belgium is the French fry capital of the world, and as one of my Belgian friends tells me, the French don't even know how to make them!

French fries really took off in America after World War I, when thousands of returning hungry American soldiers who had been stationed in Northern France and Belgium demanded them. It was there that they had first tasted and dubbed them French fries, after the French-speaking people who sold them. Today, more than 4.5 billion pounds of French fries are sold in America each year.

This whole French fry/French toast debacle reminds me of an old Rodney Dangerfield joke: "She was so wild that when she made French toast, she got her tongue caught in the toaster." I wonder if that is worse than a congressman having his foot in his mouth?

You Ate It Here First

Continuing on the absurdity shown by some congressmen over trying to punish France by changing the names of French toast and French fries, as a loyal American, I feel that it is my patriotic duty to see that our elected representatives not repeat this embarrassment. Let's make public some other locally produced firsts.

Potato Chips

Potato chips were first created and served in Saratoga Springs in 1853, just up the road from Albany and Troy. An American Indian chef (not chief) named George Crum worked at the Moon Lake Lodge's restaurant and on the menu were French-fried potatoes. To get back at a customer who didn't like the way he prepared the French fries one evening, he cut potatoes very thin and fried them to a crisp. Ironically, the customer loved them and before long everyone who came to the restaurant did too. "Saratoga Chips" became so popular that Crum opened his own restaurant. In 1932, Herman Lay, a traveling salesman from Nashville, sold chips to grocers from Atlanta to Tennessee out of the trunk of his 1929 touring car. In 1938, he bought the business and put his name on it. He became the first successfully marketed national brand of chips, and in 1961, he merged his company with the Frito Company, a Dallas-based producer of snack foods, to increase distribution. What originated as Saratoga Chips became nationally known as Lay's Brand Potato Chips. Let's be thankful, though, that they were NOT invented in Buffalo!

Coleslaw

Peter Kalm, a Swedish botanist who traveled around the world, spent some time in Albany in November 1749 and ate a special dish prepared by a Mrs. Visher who lived on Columbia Street in Albany. Here is what he described:

> *My landlady, Mrs. Visher, prepared today an unusual salad which I never remember having seen or eaten. She took the inner leaves of a head of cabbage, namely, the leaves which usually remain when the outermost leaves have been removed, and cut them in long, thin strips, about 1/12 to 1/6 of an inch wide, seldom more. When she had cut up as much as she thought necessary, she put them upon a platter, poured oil and vinegar upon them, added salt and some pepper while mixing the shredded cabbage, so that the oil etc., might be evenly distributed, as is the custom when making salads. Then it was ready.*

In place of oil, meted butter is frequently used. This is kept in a warm pot or crock and poured over the salad after it has been served. This dish has a very pleasing flavor and tastes better than one can imagine. She told me that many strangers who had eaten at her house had liked this so much that they not only had informed themselves of how to prepare it, but said that they were going to have it prepared for them when they reached their homes.

This is the first record of coleslaw, which is Dutch for "cabbage salad."

Pie a la Mode

Professor Charles Watson Townsend of Cambridge Village, just north of Troy, dined regularly at the 1885-built Cambridge Hotel in the 1930s. He often ordered ice cream with his apple pie. Mrs. Berry Hall, a diner seated next to him, asked what it was called. He said it didn't have a name, and she promptly dubbed it "pie a la mode." Townsend liked the name so much that he asked for it each day by name. When Townsend visited the famous Delmonico Restaurant in New York City, he asked for pie a la mode. When the waiter proclaimed that he never heard of it, Townsend chastised him and the manager; how could such a famous eatery not have a daily item that a small hotel in Cambridge, New York, had? The following day it became a regular at Delmonico and a resulting story in the *New York Sun* (a reporter was listening to the whole conversation) made it a country favorite with the publicity that ensued. At least that is one story.

Upon further research, we may never know the real origin of this tasty dessert. We do know that as early as June 28, 1914, in the *Miami Herald*, the Douglas' Sunday Page of Special Values listed "Pie, a'la Mode" as dessert for "Dainty Lunch Jaded Appetites." On November 20, 1920, the *Grand Forks Herald* wrote a story claiming that it was invented when a waitress carrying a few desserts tripped over a drummer's foot and ice cream fell on top of the pie, creating the first "a la mode." Regardless of the origins, we do know that it tastes great and that's all that matters really, isn't it?

Baking Powder

Finally, let's not forget the contributions by two RPI graduates. Dr. James H. Salisbury (1823–1905), a nutritionist and physician, created one of the first health diets and is famous for his Salisbury steak (which should be eaten three times a day, according to him). Eben Horsford (1818–1893) was a civil engineering student and was intrigued by the chemistry of bread and efforts to replace yeast as a leavening agent. He produced a blend of calcium acid phosphate and sodium bicarbonate, making the first commercial baking powder. It is still being made today by Rumford Baking Powder, a company that Horsford started with George F. Wilson.

The Giant Hoax

One of America's greatest scams, the Cardiff Giant, took place just south of Syracuse in the little hamlet of Cardiff in 1869. However, there is an Albany connection.

George Hull, a cigar maker/atheist from Binghamton, had argued with a revivalist minister over the passage in Genesis 6:4 that states: "There were giants in the earth in those days."

Hull went to Fort Dodge, Iowa, and obtained a multi-ton block of gypsum, which, he explained, was going to be used for a patriotic statue. The gypsum was delivered to Edward Burghardt, a stonecutter in Chicago.

Burghardt and his helpers were sworn to secrecy (with lots of beer), and they carved a massive figure of a man ten feet tall and weighing a ton and a half. Hull directed the operation to every detail, from the expression on the figure's face to the pores in his skin (created by the use of darning needles). He treated the whole structure to a bath in sulfuric acid to give it an aged look.

The giant was secretly moved to Cardiff, already famous for fossils and Indian lore, in November 1868. Hull and his brother-in-law, Stub

Newell, dug a large hole in a marshy area, covered it and planted clover on the ground. Hull went back to Binghamton to his cigar business and left the giant to "season" for a year.

On October 16, 1869, Newell hired two workmen to dig a well on his property. He directed the excavators to dig exactly where he knew the giant lay, and three feet down they uncovered the giant corpse of what they thought was a very large American Indian. Word of the discovery spread, and a tent was erected around the giant with an admission charge of fifty cents. It made Newell a small fortune, which he shared with Hull. Hundreds of people came from miles around, special stages were hired, hotels were booked and eateries made out as well.

Not everyone was convinced, however. The giant was promoted as an example of the ancient race mentioned in Genesis, proof enough for religious believers. But scientific experts offered their theories too. Dr. John F. Boynton declared that no evidence existed for the petrification of flesh and thought that it was a statue created by a Jesuit priest during the early seventeenth century to awe local Indian tribes. State Geologist James Hall from Albany was also convinced that the giant was an ancient statue and not a petrified man: "Altogether it is the most remarkable object brought to light in this country, and, although not dating back to the stone age, is, nevertheless, deserving of the attention of archaeologists." A third group said it was a hoax, but it did not stop the rising popularity of the statue.

On October 23, Newell, acting for Hull, sold three-quarters interest in the giant to five local businessmen for $30,000. On November 5, the syndicate exhumed the giant and shipped him to Syracuse to provide better surroundings. The New York Central Railroad set up a special stop for those who traveled to see it.

By November, those in the press skeptical of the whole matter began looking into Newell and Hull. Farmers remembered seeing a large crate travel toward Cardiff the prior year. Yale paleontologist Othniel C. March cracked the case when he cited fresh tool marks and smooth surfaces, and called it a "decided humbug of recent origin" in a report published November 25, 1869. Four days later, the giant was on exhibit "for a few days only" at the State Geological Hall in Albany (now State Museum).

By December 10, Hull admitted the whole story to the press.

That did not stop the public's interest, so the syndicate booked a national tour. P.T. Barnum, who tried to buy the giant for $60,000, had his own fake sculpted from wood. In December, the two were shown less than two blocks apart in New York City, and ironically, Barnum's fake outdrew the original fake.

In 1903, Mark Twain, amused by the affair, wrote "A Ghost Story," a tale about the giant's ghost that was haunting the wrong giant (it was Barnum's) while his real statue was being displayed in Albany.

Interest in the giant soon faded, and he was brought out of storage only periodically (for the 1901 Pan-American Exposition in Buffalo, and in Syracuse and Fort Dodge between 1913 and the mid-1930s).

In 1947, after being found in a rumpus room of a private home in Des Moines, Iowa, the giant was sold to the New York Historical Association for $30,000. It is now on display in a tent that duplicates the original one on the grounds of the Farmer's Museum in Cooperstown. Visitors still pay an admission charge. Barnum's fake of the fake can be seen at Marvin's Marvelous Mechanical Museum in Farmington Hills, Michigan.

PART II

Nostalgia

A Drive-In History

There's nothing like a bit of reality to spoil nostalgia. I was sitting in a '67 Mustang convertible with Margo the last time I enjoyed a drive-in movie. I can't remember the movie, but the popcorn was fresh, there were a million stars out that night and moviegoers were respectful of one another most of the time. Those were the days, during the '60s, when going to a drive-in on the weekend was the "in" thing to do. So, to jolt some of those memories back, I recently took my family to a local drive-in. More on that later.

We can thank Richard M. Hollingshead of 212 Thomas Avenue, New Jersey, for inventing drive-ins. Back in the 1920s, Hollingshead, a sales manager for his father's Whiz Auto Products Co., experimented in his driveway by hanging a sheet from some trees in his backyard to serve as a screen. With a 1928 Kodak projector on the hood of his car, he projected his test movie onto the screen.

He placed behind the screen a radio to broadcast sound. To find the best possible delivery, he experimented with the car windows up, down and even halfway. He even tested for weather conditions using his lawn sprinkler as a rainstorm.

There was one recurring problem for Mr. Hollingshead. If cars were parked behind one another, the folks in the rear cars couldn't see the entire picture. So he continued his experiments, lining up cars in his driveway and spacing them at various distances and positions. He placed blocks under the front wheels to find the correct spacing and the correct angles to build ramps for the cars to park on. On May 16, 1933, Hollingshead received patent number 1,909,537. This was the first patent for a drive-in theatre.

With an investment of $30,000, Hollingshead opened the first drive-in on Tuesday, June 6, 1933, showing *Wife Beware*, starring Adolph Menjou. The drive-in, a four-hundred-car theatre with eight rows and a thirty-by forty-foot screen, was located on Crescent Boulevard in Camden, New Jersey. Patrons paid twenty-five cents for admission for the car and twenty-five cents per person.

Unfortunately, the in-car radio speaker system was preceded by RCA Victor's "Directional Sound." Three main speakers were mounted next to the screen. It provided sound, but not of a good enough quality for cars in the rear of the theatre or neighbors who lived nearby. It would take a lawsuit against the Harper Drive-In in Detroit in 1939 to come up with the new "solo sound reproduction," the sound box in your car approach.

Between 1933 and 1939, 18 drive-ins sprouted up around the country. By 1942, there were 95 drive-ins in twenty-seven states. After World War II and the beginning of the baby boom generation in 1946, the number of drive-ins increased to 155. By 1948, there were 820 drive-in theatres across the United States. There even was a drive-in and fly-in for small planes in 1948. Ed Brown's Drive-In and Fly-In of Asbury Park, New Jersey, had a capacity for five hundred cars and twenty-five airplanes. The planes taxied into the back rows.

To win over the hearts of moviegoers new to this entertainment system, new drive-ins often would host an "open house" during the daytime, attracting as many as four hundred visitors. The owners would show customers how to park and use the sound system, and customers would marvel at the wide variety of food available in the concession stand.

Heritage on the Hudson

By the end of the decade, drive-in theatres were full of kids. Theatre owners created playgrounds in the area between the front row and the screen. Folks would often come early so the kids could play, and then the family would take a trip to the concession stand. It was a lucrative business.

The drive-in boom was on its way. By 1958, there were five thousand drive-ins, and some were huge! The Troy Drive-In in Detroit, Michigan, and the Panther Drive-In in Lufkin, Texas, held three thousand cars each! But size didn't always matter. The Harmony Drive-In in Harmony, Pennsylvania, and the Highway Drive-In in Bamberg, South Carolina, each held only fifty cars.

During this heyday of drive-ins, theatres added miniature trains, pony and boat rides, talent and animal shows, horseshoes and miniature golf. Many drive-ins would open their gates as much as three hours before the movie so customers could bring the kids early, and they began to serve a wide variety of dinners that included fried chicken, sandwiches, hamburgers and pizza, along with the usual popcorn, soda and candy. Some allowed you to order from the car and the food was delivered by a carhop.

To increase sales, the intermission trailers were invented. While they worked, they often were entertaining enough (for the kids) that one parent had to go fetch the food while the rest stayed and enjoyed (or made fun of) the trailer.

New York State was one of the first ten states to have a drive-in movie theatre. The first opened in August 1938 at Valley Stream, Long Island. The year 1963 recorded the most drive-ins in New York, with 154. In 1998, it was down to 33, the same number as in 1948, yet the state still ranked in the top ten.

How many of you remember the Super 50 Drive-In (Ballston Lake), Mohawk Drive-In (Colonie), Auto Vision Drive-In (East Greenbush), Dix Drive-In (Hudson Falls), Fort George Drive-In (Lake George), Latham Drive-In (Latham), Hudson River Drive-In (Mechanicsville), Tri City Twin Drive-In (Menands), Riverview Drive-In (Rotterdam Junction) or the Indian Ladder Drive-In (Voorheesville)? All of these are now part of history.

Yet we still have a few left in the Capital District. There's the Hollywood Drive-In in Averill Park; the Malta Drive-In in Ballston Spa; the Hi-Way Drive-In in Coxsackie; the Glen Drive-In in Glens Falls; Hathaway's Drive-In in North Hoosick; and the Jericho Drive-In in Selkirk. There are 851 drive-ins still operating in the United States.

And now to my most recent experience. I drove my family up to the unnamed drive-in and found a pretty decent spot. However, within a few minutes, several SUVs and small trucks found their spots in front of us. As their back doors sprung open and kids lit out from the back, they proceeded to get on top of the SUVs, spread their blankets and sit! I remember mumbling out loud, "I'm sure their parents are not going to let them sit on top when the movie starts. They do know that their mobile house on wheels may be a tiny bit tall for my regular-sized Subaru behind them!" In the old days, trucks and vans had to park in the REAR!

Nope, the movie started and not only did the kids sit tall, but they also whipped out their glow-in-the-dark necklaces and started whirling them around. One of the other kids, who decided to sit in the driver's seat, hit the brakes (read: brake LIGHTS) every time a scene switched. This was in between the mother who had to turn the inside lights on every time her cellphone rang (every four minutes). Three times I had to get out of the car and tell those kids to lie down. The mother was too busy talking on the cellphone.

By the way, even my kids didn't like *The Kid* or *Rocky and Bullwinkle*.

So much for nostalgia!

Nothing Finer than Diners

Do you remember eating at Gus's Diner (Bridge Diner) at Congress and River, the 5th Avenue Diner in the Burg, Miss Troy on East Side or the Palace or Sycaway Diners on Hoosick? How about the Metro on Broadway in Albany?

The Ms. Albany Diner on Broadway has been serving fine food for decades. *Courtesy of Don Rittner.*

I love eating at diners—those stainless steel boxes in Art Deco style (re: speckled Formica, linoleum and neon), the type that hold about fifty people max and have a jukebox at every table.

The old diners are stand-alone structures. One story tall and usually longer than they are wide, they often look like abandoned railroad cars or trolleys (which some are) that serve home-cooked food (and breakfast) twenty-four hours a day, cheap, and have counter service. A wise-cracking waitress is optional. They were built offsite in factories and delivered to the new owner ready to serve.

Diners dotted the American landscape from the late nineteenth century and peaked in the 1950s and '60s. While they originated in the cities, they were also located along roadsides.

Credit for the diner concept is given to Walter Scott of Providence, Rhode Island. In 1872, he began offering prepared food from a converted horse-drawn freight wagon. His nighttime lunch wagon served millworkers who could not find anything open.

In Worcester, Massachusetts, Sam Jones noticed that folks had to stand around the lunch carts to eat. So he opened a different kind of night lunch wagon in 1884. His wagon was large enough for a lunch counter with stools. His customers could come inside and sit to eat. Counters and stools became diner standards, thanks to him.

Another Worcester fellow, Thomas H. Buckley, realized that there was more money in building and selling wagons and started the first diner manufacturing company. By 1892, the New England Lunch Wagon Company had built and sold over seventy-five wagons. Buckley erected diners in over 275 towns across the country, expanding the market from the industrial Northeast, where it began.

Eventually, diner owners realized that by parking their wagons on permanent spots, they could cut down on costs (no horses to feed) and stay open longer—hence the birth of the diner as we know it today.

During the 1920s and '30s, diner manufacturers designed them to look like the sleek, cool trains of the time. Railroad food was considered a four-star meal. In fact, they are called diners because it is a shortened version of "dining car."

Since diners were mostly male oriented, due to the nature of the workforce, the owners had to rethink their strategy during the 1920s, when more women entered the workplace. Landscaping, window boxes and ornate frosted glass appeared to attract the female customers. However, women didn't want to sit on stools or at the counter (as this reminded them of bars), so diner owners installed tables down the length of the counter and promoted their "booth service." Booths became a diner standard along with the counter and stool.

Each diner was different, but folks knew you could stop at the diner and get a good meal and conversation. After all, the stool (seating a stranger) next to you was only a few inches away, and the booths not much farther. You were almost forced to be civil. If you were eating neck to neck you might as well have a chat.

The diner experience became an American staple with the introduction of the White Castle restaurants in 1921. White Castle was the first hamburger chain in America (sorry, McDonald's) and perhaps the first real fast-food franchise. Its little square hamburgers (called slyders) smothered in onions were a huge hit. Its distinctive "castle" design was memorable and the hamburger was copied.

In our area we had White Towers. These white, enameled-steel, Art Deco buildings fit maybe twenty-five people at most. They were located in Troy (Congress and Third), Menands (across from Monkey Wards), Albany (across from the Palace), Central Avenue (now the QE2, being restored) and Schenectady (State Street and Nott Terrace, recently demolished). You could get their little hamburgers for two for a quarter with a nickel coffee.

There were more than seventy-five diner builders in the 125 years since Walter Scott pushed his first food cart. Most of them were located in the Northeast, where it began. Today, there are only about half a dozen manufacturers left.

According to Diner City (www.dinercity.com), the cream of the crop were Jerry O'Mahony, Inc. (Elizabeth, New Jersey, 1913–56); Worcester Lunch Car Company (Worcester, Massachusetts, 1906–61); Silk City Diners (Paterson Vehicle Company, Paterson, New Jersey, 1927–64); Mountain View Diners (Singac, New Jersey, 1939–57); Fodero Dining Car Company (Bloomfield, New Jersey, 1933–81); Valentine Manufacturing Company (Wichita, Kansas, 1938–74); and Sterling Diners (J.B. Judkins Company, Merrimac, Massachusetts, 1936–42).

Still in existence are Paramount Diners (Oakland, New Jersey, started in 1932), DeRaffele Manufacturing Company (New Rochelle, New York, started in 1933) and Kullman Industries, Inc. (Avenel, New Jersey, started in 1927).

Unfortunately, we have lost many of our local historic diners. In Troy, the Miss Troy Diner, off Pawling Avenue, a J.G. Brill Company–built diner (1927–32), was the last to close recently (and was razed). Gus's, or the Bridge Diner, was demolished and is now a parking lot for Russell Sage. The Palace was replaced for the Collar City Bridge. The Fifth Avenue Diner is a lot. The Sycaway is now a dry cleaners. In Albany, the Metro was torn down in the 1980s.

There are thirty-seven old diners left in New York State. Fifteen are in the Capital District, according to diner historian Mike Engle from Speigletown and author of *Diners of New York* (2009, Stackpole Books). According to Mike,

Diners play a pivotal role in what America was like. They're a place for the community to come together (Dan's Place II is a perfect example). They're a dependable place to stop when you're traveling (Gibby's in Duanesburg). They're a place for truckers (Inga's and Dewey's on Fuller Rd). And they're Art. As much as some people like to see nice Brownstones, or stately city halls, they want to see a nicely preserved Diner.

Mike has been keeping count of the ones still in existence, along with noting the manufacturers of each diner he finds (they are often stamped on a metal plate somewhere in the diner). You can visit Mike's web page (www.nydiners.com/dinerbook.html) and get a rundown on the diners he has eaten at and reviewed, as well as the makers of the existing diners in our area. You can subscribe to *Roadside* magazine or visit its website at www.roadsideonline.com to learn more about existing diners around the country.

Diners may be having a comeback. Two silver diners were delivered recently: one in Guilderland (a DeRaffele) and the other in Latham Circle (a Kullman). Both seem to be doing a booming business.

Perhaps folks are tired of the hassle that goes on when you order at the "drive-thru-mundane-everything-tastes-the-same-fast-food-junk" stop and get your food delivered by a teenager who barely strings a sentence together. Maybe folks want some good old-fashioned home cooking—and a bit of conversation.

Now that I've worked up an appetite, I'm headed over to the Miss Albany. See you there.

Albany's First Road Reaches Milestone

The year 2005 marked the thirtieth anniversary of the erection of sixteen historic markers along Albany's famed King's Highway. The King's Highway was the first road between seventeenth-century Albany and Schenectady, linking the Hudson Valley to the Mohawk Valley. Although neglected in most histories, the three-hundred-year-old highway was the major trade, transportation and military route between the two valleys until 1800, and it played a major role in shaping the settlement of New York State.

Native Americans carried furs down the Mohawk Valley over a series of trails through the sandy pine barrens (called the pine bush locally) to Albany. Enterprising traders with thoughts of purchasing pelts at a minimum would wait for fur-carrying Indians on these trails, buy the furs and then resell them for a higher profit. Regulations were passed to prohibit trading outside the city gates to stop this unfair practice, but the wood runners continued and were often cited for their activities on the old path to Schenectady.

About 1663, two years after the founding of Schenectady, the "Mohagg Path" was widened from an earlier native trail into a wagon road. Albanians called it the Schenectady Path; Schenectadians called it the Albany Road. It later was simply called the King's Highway after the English conquest of the region during the later part of the seventeenth century.

The winding, sixteen-mile route crossed the pine bush, an unusual inland pine barrens environment characterized by a gently rolling topography with sand dunes and a forest of pitch pine and scrub oak. From the pine bush, and along the old road, nearby inhabitants obtained timber for building, firewood for warmth and wood for stockades. The desert-like appearance of the area impressed many travelers and depressed others on their long journey between the valleys.

In 1680, Dankers and Sluyter, two missionaries traveling to Schenectady, recorded that they "rode over a fine, sandy, cart road, through a woods of nothing but beautiful evergreen, or fir trees, but a light and barren soil." Timothy Dwight, president of Yale, passing through the region in 1798, expressed the opposite view. Dwight remarked that he "passed over a hard pine plane and presented nothing agreeable. The plain is uninhabited, the soil lean, and the road indifferent."

As trade and travel increased, several families left the protected custody of the stockaded villages and settled along the King's Highway. Few and far between, these pioneers, such as Isaac Truax and his son, operated their farms as taverns, refreshing weary travelers with food, drink and lodging. Many interesting legends and tales surround the taverns, and at one time there were taverns along the route every three to four miles. Truax was reported to be a Tory and was threatened with arrest during the American Revolution. The seven-mile house at the Verreberg was a British outpost during the French and Indian War, only to become a caretaker's house for the nearby Six Mile Waterworks in the nineteenth century.

Between 1690 and 1760, passengers traveling the old road were escorted by a patrol of Albany militiamen after reports of ambushes and scalping. The road served as a military route, as the intersection of the Hudson River with the Mohawk was blocked for boat entry by the impressive Cohoes Falls near Waterford. The King's Highway also became the point of western expansion, with roads splitting off to the west. The Palatine Germans began cutting a route to Schoharie County near the Six Mile House in 1710. The villages and towns of Guilderland, Guilderland Center, Altamont, Knox, Gallupville and Schoharie grew up along the western route. The Albany Glass Works, one of the first post–Revolutionary War industries, was built along the Palatine route in 1783. Scores of settlers traveled over the State Road, another spur off the King's Highway, constructed in 1792 near the tavern of Isaac Truax Jr.

The King's Highway did not lose its significance until the early 1800s, when the Great Western and Albany Schenectady Turnpikes were created, making it easier to move goods and people between the valleys. The construction of the Erie Canal and Mohawk and Hudson Railroad, which ran close to the King's Highway in sections, further nullified the importance of this road.

Today, the State Thruway, constructed in 1953, runs along the exact route for six thousand feet through the pine bush, and the current configuration of Albany Street in Guilderland from Old State Road into downtown Schenectady is the paved portion of this ancient highway. A mile-long section in original dirt condition still exists in the pine bush preserve.

In 1975, sixteen cast-iron markers were erected along the entire route, and this year all of them will be repainted.

Bundle Up

As a writer, I like to understand the origin of words. Take the word "bundling." Today, bundling means including software with a computer purchase. You might have childhood memories of your mom shouting, "Bundle up before you go out," or "I'll bundle you right off to bed." Well the origins of the term will give you a real surprise.

Bundling, or "tarrying," goes back to Biblical script, when Ruth and Boaz met at the threshing floor (Ruth 3). It is defined in a dictionary as "a one-time custom during courtship of unmarried couples occupying the same bed without undressing." In effect, it was the act of wrapping people together in a bed, usually as a part of courting behavior, with the aim of allowing intimacy without the possibility of sexual intercourse, and often with parental blessing. It had economic reasons too. On long, cold winter evenings, lying together under the bedcovers saved the expense of using candles and fires that would otherwise have to be lit for the couple in separate quarters.

There is an eighteenth-century poem that puts it well:

Since in a bed a man and maid,
May bundle and be chaste, It does no good to burn out wood,
It is needless waste.

There were elaborate ways to practice bundling. It is likely that a form of bundling occurred in our region, as the Dutch tradition in the Netherlands was called "queesten," a comparable word for bundling. It is described as "the singular custom of wooing, by which the doors and windows are left open, and the lover, lying or sitting outside the covering, woos the girl who is underneath." There were similar traditions in Germany, Scandinavia, England and other parts of the Old World. In fact, the Oxford English Dictionary defines bundling as early as 1781.

It certainly occurred in colonial America and in particular in Pennsylvania and New England. It was a common custom among the poor and rural folks, where beds were in scarce supply, not to mention the firewood needed to heat at night. Bundling was not confined to lovers in courtship either. Army officers, doctors, candidates for office and even the minister were invited to join the family. The idea was that if both people were "bundled"—that is, fully clothed—chances of anything happening were reduced.

Not everyone thought it was moral, especially many in the religious arena. Poems and sermons were written against it, as well as those written in favor. Some households used "centerboards"—slabs of wood that separated the two lovebirds, at least in theory. Bundling was advertised as a way to let single males know that a single female was available. Mothers would put a bundling candle in the window and the "date" would enter through the window.

In New York, bundling was known as "questing," probably a derivative of the Dutch "queesten." Washington Irving (Diedrich Knickerbocker), in his *History of New York*, humorously describes: "To this sagacious custom, therefore, do I chiefly attribute the unparalleled increase of the Yanokie or Yankee tribe; for it is a certain fact, well authenticated by court records and parish registers, that wherever the practice of bundling prevailed, there was an amazing number of sturdy brats annually born unto the state, without the license of the law, or the benefit of clergy."

We know from Jonathan Pearson in his 1883 *History of Schenectady Patent* that bundling was performed locally. Pearson states that while the Dutch here kept males and females apart in church, they did not elsewhere, and in fact he talks a great deal about bundling. He goes on to mention,

> *From Notarial Papers of Albany and other sources, tradition being the most prolific as well as the most uncertain, "bundling" was common in the early days along the whole of both sides of the Hudson River and in all the settlements of the back country. As civilization advanced the practice grew into desuetude and along the great highways of travel it had become uncommon before the close of the last century in the cities and towns of this vicinity.*

Pearson goes on to say, "In Albany it was said to be a custom along the Mohawk. At Schenectady no one is old enough to remember it as nearer than the Catskills, Helderbergs and Schoharie and German Flats. It is difficult to say where the people there locate it. It is like malaria, always over in the next valley."

Pearson also discusses a few court cases that discussed bundling in Albany and Orange Counties in 1804. In an 1853 case, *Graham v. Smith*, witnesses testified that the practice was a universal custom and one fifty-six-year-old woman said that it had been a custom since she was a kid. Pearson also says that in 1853 it was still being practiced in the backcountry.

There is a record of a young Albany lady in 1658 whose reputation was well known, and in court the principal witness testified that "when we were visiting together, we slept together in the garret," and also stated that the lady was "perfectly virtuous," a clear example of bundling.

Even in puritanical New England, where it was considered rude for a man to even mention a woman's leg or knee, it was thought quite civil to ask her to bundle. Often bundling bags (forerunner of today's sleeping bags), pillows and bolsters were used to separate the two. One Connecticut woman was forced by her mother to put both legs in a pillowcase and tie it around her waist. The next morning, the innocent maid proclaimed to her mother that everything had gone well and she had only taken one leg out during the evening!

In 1937, a magazine published a picture of a married couple in bed, separated by a heavy plank that had twenty-penny spikes driven in toward the wife's side. She went to court for a divorce on the grounds of cruelty. There are numerous funny and not so funny accounts of bundling.

Bundling was known to occur in Pennsylvania as late as 1933 and New Jersey in 1938. On December 12, 1969, *Time* magazine featured an article on the Society to Bring Back Bundling, which had been formed in Pottstown, Pennsylvania.

Today, we have the automobile, theatres (drive-ins) and the mall as places of courtship. And if you think bundling is history, watch a few episodes of MTV's *Real World*, or follow the antics of Michael Jackson.

As for me, the only bundles I want to see have pictures of George Washington on them!

Minding Our Manors

It's hard to imagine that the entire Capital District was under the ownership of the Van Rensselaer family and their feudal land system for some three hundred years. Yet, there are a few standing structures scattered about the region to remind us.

Certainly the manor houses in which the families lived in on both sides of the Hudson were imposing structures. In 1765, Stephen Van Rensselaer erected his manor house near present-day Manor Street in Albany's north end. The manor house underwent several renovations between the years 1840 and 1843. Toward the end of the century, the estate was getting crowded with the growing railway system in Albany. Soon after the death of Stephen Van Rensselaer IV in 1868, the house was handed down to the next generation of the Van Rensselaer family, who chose not to reside there, since it was then in the middle of an industrial center.

The East Manor House called Beverwyck was built in 1842 by William Patterson Van Rensselaer, the son of Stephen III and inheritor of most of Rensselaer County. It has been owned by the Conventual Franciscan Friars of the Immaculate Conception Province and used as St Anthony's on the Hudson Friary for years. *Courtesy of Don Rittner.*

The Van Rensselaer Palace on State Street in Albany. *Courtesy Don Rittner.*

The Van Rensselaer insignia on a building at the corner of Madison and Lark Streets in Albany. *Courtesy of Don Rittner.*

The Van Rensselaer Manor House in North Albany before being dismantled. *Courtesy of the Library of Congress.*

Owner William Bayard Van Rensselaer decided to remove one wing of the house to make room for the New York Central Railroad, but his cousin, Marcus T. Reynolds, an Albany architect, convinced him that it would be better to remove the house completely rather than alter it. Much of it was removed and it became Reynolds's fraternity house, Sigma Phi, at Williams College in Massachusetts. Historical interior details of the manor house—including the now famous wallpaper that was ordered especially made for the manor house and saved by William's brother, Dr. Howard Van Rensselaer—were given to the Metropolitan Museum of Art in New York. Much of the brick walls was used to fill in the cellar hole. Today, the site is a parking lot.

Construction at Williams College was completed and the Van Rensselaer Sigma Phi house opened in 1895. In 1963, fraternities were abolished and the manor house was used for various purposes until 1973, when the college demolished it to extend its library. A Dr. Demise from the capital region salvaged the original sandstone blocks that were used in the 1840s renovations, under direction of the famous architect Richard Henry Upjohn, and moved them to a farm in Feura Bush in 1973. The blocks are now in two places: partially in a landfill, while the quoins and lintels were dumped at the RPI technology park in 1997.

In 1893, William organized the Albany Terminal Warehouse Company to obtain additional income for the family, and a large warehouse was erected on their property across the alley from the manor house. The warehouse is still being used today.

Another Van Rensselaer building is the beautiful Venetian Renaissance–style palace designed by Marcus Reynolds at 385–389 State Street across from Washington Park. Built by William in 1896 with family money, it was built as a retirement home for any of the Van Rensselaer family who wanted to live there. If you look carefully at the terra cotta plaques on the front, you can see above the second-floor arched windows the main emblem of the Van Rensselaer coat of arms (called a Cross Moline), originally discovered by historian John Wolcott.

The third Albany building of the Van Rensselaers, again attributed to Marcus Reynolds, is on the southeast corner of Delaware and Madison Avenues. This building was built around the turn of the twentieth century and financed by Dr. Howard Van Rensselaer. If you look at the hand-wrought balustrade over the door, you can see the very ornate monogram "VR" in the middle. Reynolds always liked to use these low-key reminders of the Van Rensselaer connections in his projects.

Though the West Manor house has been destroyed, minus the few architectural elements scattered around, the East Manor house did not suffer the same fate. It was built in 1842 by William Patterson Van Rensselaer, the son of Stephen III and inheritor of most of Rensselaer County. The building is as elegant today as it was when originally built. This massive Greek Revival structure is located off Washington Avenue in Rensselaer on beautiful wooded grounds and overlooks the Hudson. According to Wolcott, William P. named it Beverwyck as a reminder that his family had really founded Albany. It has been owned by the Conventual Franciscan Friars of the Immaculate Conception Province and used as St. Anthony's on the Hudson Friary for years.

Few know that William also commissioned Thomas Cole, who is generally considered the father of the American Hudson River School, to paint two paintings for him in 1837. Cole produced the now famous *The Departure* and *The Return*.

William sold his Rensselaer County land to his brother, Stephen Van Rensselaer IV. Stephen is credited with starting the famous anti-rent wars by getting all the tenant farmers mad for leaning on them harshly to collect back rent money due to his bad gambling debts in the 1830s. The land empire crumbled shortly after.

The rest is history, in a "manor" of speaking.

Albany's Other Mascot

My friend and colleague Paul Grondahl wrote a wonderful story in the *Times Union* about Albany's Owney, the stray Scottish terrier and post office mascot who rode the mail trains and boats around the world.

Albany has another canine mascot that towers above Owney—at least in size. If you haven't noticed that large dog sitting on top of a downtown

RCA's Nipper still looking down from the old RCA building on Broadway in Albany. *Courtesy of the Library of Congress.*

Broadway building, well you simply don't see very well. Nipper may just be a bit more famous than Owney!

Nipper is best known as the advertising trademark "RCA Dog," but he started as a real mutt in Bristol, England, as part bull terrier and fox terrier.

Nipper was a stray in Bristol, England, and was rescued in 1884 by Mark Barraud, a Bristol theatre stage set painter. When Mark died in 1887, his brother, photographer and painter Francis Barraud, adopted the small mutt (named for his attraction to nip people's ankles). Francis often noticed that when he was listening to his Edison-Bell cylinder phonograph (yes kids, way before digital CDs), he noticed that the mutt was listening with his head cocked, trying to figure out where the voice was coming from. He thought perhaps Nipper was trying to listen for his first owner's voice.

Nipper was eventually given to his brother's widow, and the dog died in 1895. Remembering the image of Nipper and the phonograph, Francis decided to paint the image. It was finished on February 11, 1899, and he titled it *Dog looking at and listening to a Phonograph*. It was later changed to *His Master's Voice*.

Inspired by his painting, Francis took it to Edison-Bell and offered to sell it, but a company spokesman complained that dogs didn't listen to phonographs and the painting was too dark. Francis visited a new company called Gramophone in London's Maiden Lane to borrow a new bright brass horn and include the lighter horn in the painting. After showing the painting to the manager, Barry Owen, Owen asked Francis if he could redo the picture with their Gramophone instead of the Edison version. He took the new Berliner "Improved Gramophone" and painted it on top of the existing one. Owen offered him £100 ($167): £50 for the painting and the other £50 for the copyright. In England, the trademark was called *Dog and Trumpet*.

By the time Barraud died on August 29, 1924, he had been commissioned to make twenty-four more copies of the painting.

Emile Berliner used the painting as his logo in the United States, and when Eldridge Johnson, who formed the Victor Talking Machine Company, acquired his company, Nipper became the most famous dog in the world. Johnson received a U.S. patent for *His Master's Voice* instead of *Dog and Trumpet* on July 10, 1909, and this image came to represent RCA Victor for years. RCA purchased the Victor Talking Machine Company in 1929; however, RCA tossed the Nipper logo in the '60s for a new look.

In the merger mania years of the 1980s, General Electric bought the RCA Victor Company (it owned RCA before 1932 but sold it) and sold the home entertainment division to Thomson Consumer Electronics. Thomson decided to introduce a new trademark, Nipper and his younger companion, Chipper, a Jack Russell terrier, in 1991. Unfortunately for them, they have to keep replacing Chipper since the dogs keep growing up.

The current living Nipper has his own limo. The first Nipper has a plaque on his grave.

Albany's four-ton, twenty-five-foot-high Nipper, created out of fiberglass composite over a steel mesh frame supported by ironwork, was erected in 1954 with horn and box on 991 Broadway. Only Nipper remains today. Other RCA distributors had Nippers on top at some point, but Albany's is the largest and may be the lone survivor. Fortunately, the current owner of the building, Arnoff Moving and Storage Building, has recognized the landmark and is leaving it in place. In fact, it has become a new trademark of sorts, with Arnoff using the slogan, "The watchdog of your possessions."

There is more to the story. Our Nipper has a part of history that no other Nipper has. He sits and looks over the intersection of Broadway and the beginning of Niskayuna Road. This is the same winding road that runs northwest up to old Niskayuna to the end of Burhmaster Road on the Mohawk River. It is the road on which Simon Schermerhorn rode on February 8, 1690, into Albany's North Gate at 5:00 a.m. to warn Albanians of the Schenectady Massacre and impending attack on Albany.

I would bet that if Nipper had been sitting at Schenectady's gate, the French and Indians might have thought otherwise.

Happy Birthday Albany

Many of you know that the city of Albany celebrated a big 350th anniversary in 2002. It was on April 10, 1652, that the official directive was given establishing the government of the village of Beverwyck. A yearlong series of events took place to commemorate this anniversary. We skeptics were a bit puzzled at all this celebration, as it appears that the city's policy when it finds important archaeological sites of that same period is to bury them with office buildings and parking facilities. I guess the attitude is "let's celebrate it but don't ask us to save any of this stuff"!

A couple of years ago, Albany historian John Wolcott and yours truly penned a new Albany Plan of Preservation, modeled after Ben Franklin's Albany Plan of 1754. History buffs will recall that Franklin met in Albany on Broadway with representatives of all the colonies and the League of the Iroquois (at their request) to form one speaking voice, in effect, creating the "United" States of America. Okay, our plan wasn't as far reaching, but we felt that the city did indeed need some plan to address the mess it kept getting into—that is, finding very important archaeological sites after plans have been finalized for office buildings and parking garages. We thought we would show the city, at no charge, how to have its cake and eat it too. The mayor told me that he read our plan. Well at least we accomplished that!

Part of our plan called for the establishment of a Beverwyck Archaeological Park, and we still think it's a great idea. What is known today as the D&H Plaza at the intersection of Broadway and State was, at one time before 1914, very much the heart of early Albany. Much earlier, in the seventeenth to early nineteenth centuries, the Dutch church sat in the middle of the street and small Dutch gabled houses surrounded it on all sides, down Broadway and up and down State (lower State no longer exists). That section of Albany evolved through the nineteenth and twentieth centuries, and in 1913–15, the entire area was demolished to construct the D&H building and plaza in front of it. Broadway was much narrower than today.

Dutch gable home at 674 Broadway in Albany (demolished) of the seventeenth or early eighteenth century. With Flemish brick bond and fleur-de-lis wall ties, this was a typical Dutch American house of the period. *Courtesy of the Library of Congress.*

Three original stockade posts from Albany, perhaps from the 1680s–90s. *Courtesy of John Wolcott.*

The archaeological park would consist of all the area in front of the D&H building and up to the original line of Broadway. What's under there? Well, probably the foundations of many of the earliest Albany settlers. That includes the Stadt Huys ("city house"). This building was the center for Albany's regional government, which included Albany, Schenectady, Niskayuna, Half Moon, Catskill and Kinderhook, and was created when the British administration took over the area in 1664. It was also called the "Coenings Huys" or "King's House." To the Mohawks, and likely the Mohicans, it was very important because it was the locale of many of their conferences with colonial officials. The leader of the Maquaas (Mohawks) made a speech in this house in 1689 at the opening of King William's War, when the English were seeking their alliance against the French. Oh yeah, it's also where Ben Franklin presented his "Plan" in the rebuilt and enlarged building of 1740.

Also buried there is Peter Schuyler's house. Schuyler bought the house in 1679 and was the first mayor of Albany under the charter of 1686. What else? Probably three of the defensive walls that protected Albany—the plank wall of 1659 and the stockades of 1698 and 1756 and others in between, as well as the South Gate of the Stockade, probably circa 1671. Also, there were two seventeenth-century houses of William Loveridge, master hatter. The northern one was converted to, or replaced by, a brew house by the end of the century. There were also homes of Jochim Wessels, the baker (in back of his house were held illegal Lutheran services that were banned by Peter Stuyvesant), and Jurriaem Teunisse, the glassmaker, to name a few.

The entire plaza could be excavated to reveal these sites and others and could be totally enclosed, similar to the museum in Montreal. Additionally, this could be connected to the area south of it where portions of the original Fort Orange probably survive under Broadway. There is even the chance that remains of some of the earliest houses that were built right outside the fort are still there.

The result? A world-famous heritage tourist attraction. Now, if you think our idea is far-fetched, there is another one floating out there, more destructive than productive. It's a canal running in front of the D&H building, taking up all of Broadway. There is one thing I'm sure of, and that's that Albany ain't no Venice.

Up Against the (City) Wall

Many ancient towns, cities and even countries around the world were fortified with walls to protect their citizens from enemy attack. Perhaps the most famous is the two-thousand-year-old Great Wall of China that stretches for 4,500 miles. Romans in the third century built walls around most of their major cities because of increasing threats of invasion from the northern "barbarians." Today, there are currently 131 walled towns and cities in twenty-three countries in Europe and beyond that have protected their historic walls and fortifications.

Here in America, Iroquois and Mohican villages were surrounded by wooden walls called stockades, made from pitch pines and other trees, as were the early settlements of Albany and Schenectady. Troy was not fortified; it wasn't settled until after the Revolution. However, other early American cities like Savannah, Georgia, Charleston, South Carolina, and St. Augustine, Florida, were all walled. How did New York City's Wall Street get its name? It too had a stockade built in 1653 by Dutch colonists to protect the settled area south of it from attack.

Most walls were made from timber because it was cheaper to cut the trees down, although they were high maintenance. As the city grew, expanding the fortification was accomplished simply by moving the existing wall or building a new one. This occurred in Albany several times. There were stockades erected in 1659 (actually a plank wall), 1698 and 1756. Throughout the intervening years, rotten timbers were replaced as needed. In fact, Beverwyck/Albany passed a law stating that people could not rent building lots outside the wall until all the building lots inside were filled up because of the expense of moving the wall.

In Canada, Quebec City is famous for being the only city in North America to have an existing "stone" wall around it, and thousands of visitors flock there each year to shop. Albany would also be surrounded by a stone wall if it and the New York Provincial Legislature weren't so cheap in the eighteenth century. In fact, Albany did build part of a stone wall, and it may still be lying under the ground waiting to be rediscovered (and then buried with a new parking garage, which appears to be the fate of all Albany archaeology projects).

Part of the original Albany Stockade near Dock Street during construction of a parking garage in 2006. *Courtesy of Don Rittner.*

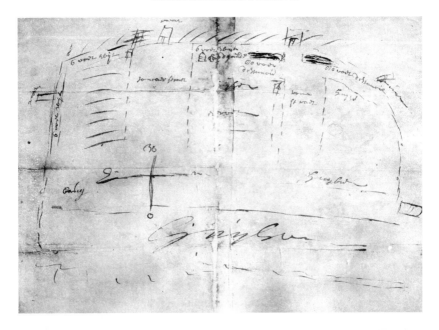

An Albany map (actually a builder's sketch) showing the first stockade surrounding the village, dated 1659, by historian John Wolcott. This shows horizontal planks rather than vertical posts typical of the later stockade wall. *Courtesy of John Wolcott.*

Albany's stone wall, built in 1734 near what is today the north side of Orange Street. *Courtesy of John Wolcott.*

Heritage on the Hudson

In September 1733, Albany officials petitioned Governor William Cosby for permission to assess the city and county inhabitants to improve their fortifications, "as we are seated on the frontiers of this province and have very dangerous neighbors to the northward who have made encroachments on us."

The following year, Albany started constructing a stone wall, but also petitioned the governor for new wooden stockades until the stone wall was completed. For some reason, Albany only constructed a stone section along the north, 334 feet long, from the river to the road to Watervliet, present-day Broadway.

Albany's stone wall tapered as it rose ten and a half feet in the air. There were evenly spaced holes for rifles and muskets eight feet high (implying a wooden firing platform). A map of the wall was drawn by John Montressor, British military engineer in the 1760s.

Why the wall was not completed is unknown. It may be that the city decided not to go ahead with it, considering the expense, even though in 1753, it petitioned for a tax on everyone in the county to try to finish it, referring to the still standing "stone wall begun several years ago." Albany County was then all the settled land above Ulster County.

It was clear by 1755 that construction of the stone wall wasn't going to happen, and officials petitioned instead for the inhabitants to be required to provide regular timber stockades. In 1762, the area behind the stone wall was dubbed Wall Street, now present-day Orange Street. And so Albany's big plan for a walled city of stone crumbled. A resolution was passed in 1768 to dismantle and use the stone for a north dock. Only archaeology can determine if the lower foundation courses of the great stone wall and a possible moat are still there.

Ironically, this fortified mentality has come back in a newer package. Since the 1980s, new gated communities have been springing up around the country. Millions of Americans have chosen to live in walled and fenced communal residential space. By using gates, fences, private security guards, video surveillance, exclusionary land-use policies, tighter development regulations and other planning tools, we are increasingly restricting access to residential, commercial and public spaces.

Who are we afraid of this time?

Albany's Revered Scientist

Perhaps no other scientist to this day was revered as much as Albany-born Joseph Henry, yet he is little known among today's public.

Joseph, the son of teamster William Henry and Ann Alexander, was born in Albany in 1797, the year Albany became the capital of New York. Of Scottish descent, his father, an alcoholic, died when Joseph was thirteen, and Joseph spent much of his youth living with his grandmother in nearby Galway.

Self-educated, Henry was accepted to the Albany Academy, a private boys' school that opened only seven years after his birth but was to be instrumental in his science career. He attended the academy between 1819 and 1822, while in his twenties, and became a professor of mathematics and natural philosophy (physics) at the academy in 1826.

Besides teaching, Henry pursued his interest in experimental science at the academy, which brought him national recognition through his original research on electromagnetics. A year after he began teaching, Henry presented his first paper on October 10, 1827, at the Albany Institute.

Henry discovered mutual electromagnetic induction—the production of an electric current from a magnetic field—and electromagnetic self-induction independently of England's Michael Faraday.

During the early 1830s, Henry constructed some of the most powerful electromagnets, an oar separator, a prototype telegraph and the first electric motor. He also is given credit for encouraging Alexander Graham Bell's invention of the telephone.

Henry built a 21-pound "Albany magnet" that supported 750 pounds, making it the most powerful magnet ever constructed at the time. He described his experiments in a paper published in the *American Journal of Science*, a widely read and influential publication, in January 1831.

In 1832, Henry began teaching at Princeton and continued his work in electromagnetism, but also turned to the study of auroras, lightning, sunspots, ultraviolet light and molecular cohesion. His interest in meteorology began in Albany while collecting weather data and compiling reports of statewide meteorological observations for the State

Albany's Joseph Henry, first secretary of the Smithsonian and inventor of the electromagnet and electric motor. *Courtesy of the Library of Congress.*

A stained-glass window depicting Joseph Henry at the First Presbyterian Church in Albany. *Courtesy of Don Rittner.*

University with T.R. Beck, principal of Albany Academy. Ironically, it was Beck who convinced Henry to attend the academy, countering an offer from the Albany Green Street Theater, where Henry was pursuing an encouraging acting career.

In 1846, Henry was elected secretary of the newly established Smithsonian Institute, which he guided until his death. He was instrumental in fostering research in a variety of disciplines, including anthropology, archaeology, astronomy, botany, geophysics, meteorology and zoology.

One of his first priorities as head of the Smithsonian was to set up "a system of extended meteorological observations for solving the problem of American storms." Henry began creating the national weather service. By 1849, he had a budget of $1,000 and a network of some 150 volunteer weather observers. Ten years later, the project had more than 600 volunteers, including people in Canada, Mexico, Latin America and the Caribbean.

The Smithsonian supplied volunteers with instructions, standardized forms and instruments. The volunteers submitted monthly reports that included observations on temperature, barometric pressure, humidity, wind, cloud conditions and precipitation levels. Comments were also solicited on events such as thunderstorms, hurricanes, tornadoes, earthquakes, meteors and auroras.

In 1861, the first of a two-volume compilation of climatic data and storm observations, based on the volunteers' reports for the years 1854–59, was published.

Henry's observations of weather patterns or storms, moving west to east, gave him the idea in 1847 that he could use telegraphy to warn the northern and eastern parts of the country on advancing storms, giving rise to weather forecasting.

By 1857, Henry had a number of telegraph companies transmitting weather data for free to the Smithsonian. To gain an overview of this information, Henry created a large daily weather map to show weather conditions across the country. In 1856, this map was displayed in the Smithsonian for the public to view and became a popular attraction. By May 1857, Henry shared the information with the *Washington Evening Star*, which began publishing daily weather conditions, giving rise to the now daily weather page. His map also allowed some forecasting ability, but his plan to predict storm warnings to the East Coast was squashed with the advent of the Civil War. After the war, Henry wrote in his annual report in 1865 that the federal government should establish a national weather service to predict weather conditions. In 1870, Congress put storm and weather predictions in the hands of the U.S. Army's Signal Service, and in 1874, Henry convinced the Signal Service to absorb his volunteer observer system. In 1891, the newly created U.S. Weather Bureau (now National Weather Service) took over the weather functions of the Signal Service.

Henry directed the Smithsonian for nearly thirty-two years, and when he died, the government closed for his funeral on May 16, 1878; it was attended by the president, vice president, the cabinet, the members of the Supreme Court, Congress and the senior officers of the army and the navy.

After his death, Alexander Graham Bell arranged for Henry's wife Harriet to have free phone service out of his appreciation for Henry's early encouragement.

In 1893, the International Congress of Electricians named the international unit of inductance "the henry" in his honor. More than a dozen items have been named in his honor.

Paying by the Mile

By Revolutionary War times, there were about a dozen people living in the Troy area. If you lived here at the time, all roads led to Troy—sort of. Actually, there were only two roads and they both ended at the house of Derrick Vanderheyden at the corner of present-day Ferry and River.

One road went north, following most of the course of present-day River Street, and then split, with one end continuing north into Pleasantdale and the other going east up to Schagticoke. North First Street from King Street to North Street follows this path today and may be the only original part of this historic road left. The second road from Vanderheyden's house went northeast to Hoosick.

For years, Vanderheyden or tenants to whom he leased ran a ferry here, and it was the only way to cross the river. Farmers from the Bought area (Cohoes) just west of here found it easier to bring their produce here instead of Albany or Lansingburgh. But there were other markets in Vermont, Massachusetts and beyond that would prove profitable to whoever monopolized that trade with good roads.

Elkanah Watson helped stir up the issue of road improvements in the entire Capital District region. Watson, an Albanian who believed in good infrastructure, was a supporter of the growing turnpike movement—toll roads owned by corporations. The turnpike idea wasn't new. Britain first authorized a toll road in 1663, and "turnpike mania" swept England from about 1750 to 1772.

When a turnpike organizer in Albany couldn't get public interest aroused, Watson wrote a series of articles in the Troy and Albany

Four-milestone of the Northern Turnpike to Lansingburgh. *Courtesy of Don Rittner.*

This milestone (mile ten) for the Albany-Schenectady Turnpike was located near the Stanford Mansion in Schenectady. *Courtesy of Don Rittner.*

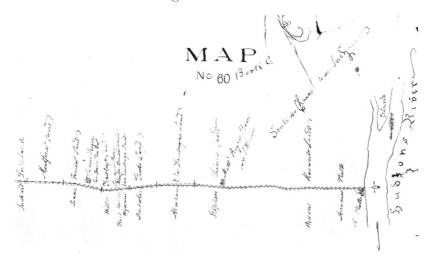

A portion of the 1806 map of the Troy-Schenectady Turnpike by Lawrence Vrooman. *Courtesy of the Efner Research Library.*

newspapers baiting each other. In the Albany paper, he chastised the readers for letting Lansingburgh and Troy attempt to monopolize the northern trade at their expense. In the Troy paper, he encouraged Trojans to build a turnpike connecting to Schenectady on the west to compete with Albany. Additional articles finally produced the desired effect. Albanians were jealous and fearful that Troy would steal all the northern trade, and the Schenectady Turnpike Company was created. Lansingburgh wasn't sleeping either.

In 1799, Albany developed the Great Western Turnpike (present Western Avenue). Lansingburgh followed with the Northern Turnpike (starting at the southwest corner of 124th Street and 4th Avenue), and directly across from Albany in Rensselaer the Eastern Turnpike and Rensselaer-Columbia (originally called the Albany-Columbia in 1798) Turnpike were created.

By 1805, there were several turnpikes radiating out from the Albany and Troy area.

Troy finally created the Troy-Schenectady Turnpike in 1802 and Albany followed with the Albany and Schenectady Turnpike, also in 1802, and the Albany-Delaware in 1805. Whatever Albany did, Troy was sure to follow—or vice versa.

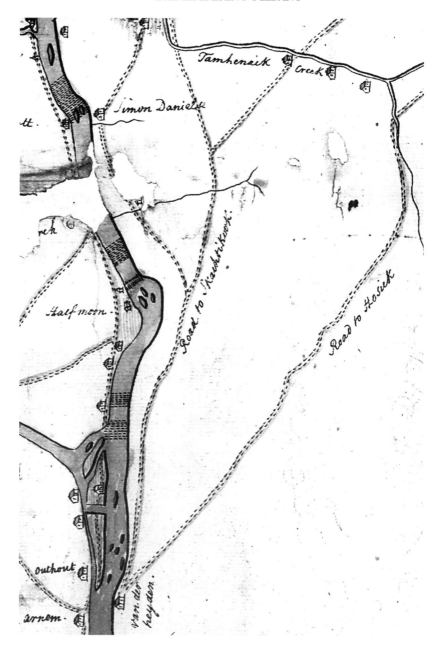

Map of Albany, circa 1760, showing two roads leading from the Vanderheyden Home.
Courtesy of the Library of Congress.

Although New York was almost last in terms of states promoting the turnpike (New York's full adoption of the turnpike plan came only with its general law in 1807), the infrastructure for trade routes, along with river transportation, was now in place for the Capital District region.

Turnpikes, however, were not the financial windfall that supporters thought they would be. Most were unprofitable, not to mention unwelcomed by local citizenry (who often used free roads called "shunpikes" to get around the toll gates).

From 1797 through 1846, 449 turnpike companies were incorporated in New York State but the number of those turnpike companies that actually built roadways and collected tolls was only 165. Even the short-lived boom of plank roads between 1846 and 1853 didn't help (Fifth Avenue in the Burgh was a plank road).

Water routes (Hudson River and the Erie Canal) and later steam (steam powerboats and trains) would kill the turnpikes eventually, but these two factors would help Troy stand out from the rest.

You can still find remnants of the toll roads in the area since they were marked by stone mile markers showing you how far you were from your destination. There is a great Northern Turnpike marker on the way to Schagitcoke (corner of Route 40 and Fogarty Road, Speigletown). The Delaware Turnpike (Delaware Avenue) in Albany to New Scotland has several of its milestones still in place.

A tollhouse was located at both ends of the toll roads and here you paid a toll, normally a few cents. All of the tollhouses in the Capital District are gone.

When the movement to build bridges began, they also charged tolls, and this practice was still in effect in the early part of the twentieth century. Many old-timers tell me that they paid to walk across the old Green Island bridge. Of course, any of you who drive down the Thruway know that some ideas, no matter how good or bad, never die.

The City with a Beat

You are eligible for an AARP card if you have ever heard of the Ruins, Blotto, Bougaloo, Monolith, OD, Horton Strong, Love's Ice Cubes, Tino and the Revlons or The Knickerbockers.

While it may be hard to imagine, Troy and Albany have quite a music history, and it didn't begin with the 1960s. In fact, original music has been written and recorded in Troy for close to two hundred years.

The Troy Music Hall, famous for its acoustics, was opened on April 19, 1875. Even before the city was a city, members of the Apollo Lodge, Free and Accepted Masons, purchased a bassoon, violin and other instruments to form a band in 1797.

The Schenectady Museum had an exhibit on the history of local music, called "Factory Bands to Funk Music in the Capital Region, 1900 to Present," at its Nott Terrace location. Part of the exhibit featured photographs and information on several local company bands. It seems that during the early part of the twentieth century, many companies like General Electric, American Locomotive and Mohawk Carpet Mills

The 1970s rock group Horton Strong at the Saratoga Performing Arts Center in 1972. *Courtesy of Don Rittner.*

sponsored or initiated small bands that played local gigs. These probably instilled camaraderie among the workers and a sense of connection with the companies they worked for. Also viewable in the exhibit were some interesting early instruments, including an odd-looking Gibson-made harp-guitar hybrid. Costumes, bandstands and a room with mood music "atmosphere" allowed you to sit and do some contemplation.

Over at the other end of the museum was a section that contained many locally produced 45 rpm records by local groups with names like The Units (Fear of Strangers), The Distraction, Coal Palace Kings, Stomplistics, Working Class Stiffs and others. Other memorabilia, such as broadsides and other PR pieces, along with photos of the bands, were on exhibit.

To make it really interactive, the exhibit contained a full drum set, an organ and a xylophone-type instrument (made with cardboard or plastic pipes) that visitors could play. Part of the exhibit featured live performances by local musicians such as Ernie Williams, Ruth Pelham, the Uncle Sam Chorus and over a dozen more.

It was a real walk down memory lane when I viewed the material dealing with the '60s and '70s. As anyone who grew up here will tell you, Troy and Albany had a great music scene. In Troy, rock bands played at RPI and its fraternities, Paul's, Valenti's on West Sand Lake Road and early on at the Escape, the basement of a church on Hoosick Street. In Albany, Bogart's, J.B. Scotts and Refer Network's Sunday concerts in Washington Park were favorites. Other venues included the College Inn up toward Saratoga and the Hide Out in Glenmont.

Several local groups had their music recorded, including the Bougaloo, Tino, The Knickerbockers and Blotto, and others like Horton Strong had their original music played on local radio stations. If you were an aspiring musician, you purchased your instruments at Hilton's (Troy and Albany), Romeo's or George's Music Store. If you wanted to actually learn how to read music or take lessons, you would go over to Miller's Music Store on Fourth Street.

RPI's radio station, WRPI, used to have a live performance night, and singers like Natalie Merchant would stop by (before she made it big). On Saturday nights, you would tune in to *Kaleidoscope* with Jim Barrett—

who still does *Kaleidoscope* on WZMR, 104.9 FM—and the commercial stations like WTRY and WPTR with jocks like Lee Gray and Boom Boom Brannigan would spin out the top forty hits.

Most of us rock and roll wannabes never made it big, of course, but it sure was fun trying. In those days, getting a record contract was not easy. There was no such thing as digital music, just analog. You bought vinyls, not CDs, and having stereo meant that you had two speakers.

Today, groups can make their own digital music, some without actual instruments, using software like Apple's Garageband. They press their own CDs from their personal computers and market their homemade product on the Internet or at their gigs. You can now download music from Apple computer into your iPod for ninety-nine cents a song and store over one thousand songs.

As Bob Dylan once sang, "The times they are a-changing."

History Is a Knick of Time

One of my favorite local historic sites is the Knickerbocker Mansion in Schaghticoke (Algonquian for "meeting of the waters"). The mansion is under the care and restoration of the Knickerbocker Historical Society, a determined and motivated group of volunteers that rescued it from certain demolition. It's also the site where a great legend associated with the Hudson Valley and New York originated.

This ancient mansion, surrounded by cornfields and just south of the Hoosic River off Knickerbocker Road, was the home of the Knickerbocker family for some 250 years. It was Washington Irving ("Dietrich Knickerbocker") who forever branded the Knickerbocker name with the Dutch history of New York State. His relationship with New York congressman Herman Knickerbocker (affectionately called the "Prince of Schaghticoke"), and the whole Knickerbocker family, may be the model for Irving's now famous satirical history of New York. At a recent visit to the mansion, it was easy to imagine the two of them trading stories. (Herman was known as a prankster.)

The Knickerbocker Mansion. The Knickerbocker family that lived here may have served as the model for Washington Irving's now famous satirical history of New York. *Courtesy of Don Rittner.*

The Knickerbocker site in Schaghticoke was settled about 1700. Harmen Jansen van Wyhe came to America and started the Knickerbocker line, although it was his great-grandson, Johannes, who built the current mansion about 1770. Harmen was born about 1648, arriving in America about 1674. He called himself "van Wyekycback(e)," using that name on a land contract in 1682. He is the ancestor of all Knickerbockers in North America.

The origin of the name Knickerbocker (or Knickerbacker) is still a matter of conjuncture, but regardless, it became synonymous with New York's Dutch history and was made famous by Irving. Irving's "history" of 1809 combined fact with fiction. His now famous homestead, Sunnyside, in Tarrytown, New York, is also a combination of real and imaginary. He somehow "borrowed" or purchased several items from the old Vanderheyden Palace in Albany before it was torn down.

The Vanderheyden Palace was next to Philip Livingston's house on North Pearl and was built in 1725 by Johannes Beeckman. In 1778, it was purchased by one of Troy's Vanderheydens. The palace became the "residence of Heer Anthony Vanderheyden," in the 1822 setting of Irving's *Bracebridge Hall*, the story of Dolph Heyliger. It's clear that Irving had affection for the place since he obtained the running horse weather vane and date irons from the building, and it is reported that one of the gable ends of the house was also taken. All of these items were reused at Sunnyside.

There is also an odd connection between Irving, Albany and the Knickerbocker Mansion. Next to the Vanderheyden Palace, at Philip Livingston's house, Livingston, one of the signers of the Declaration of Independence, planted a symbolic elm tree. The tree lived for 123 years before it was taken down on June 15, 1877. Over at the Knickerbocker Mansion, to reconvene their friendship with the settlers, around one thousand Native Americans met at the site of the Knickerbocker Mansion in 1676 and signed a peace treaty. It was sealed with the planting of a symbolic oak peace tree, or "tree of welfare," called the *Witenagemot* (Old English for "meeting of wise men"; historically, a session of the counselors of a king in Anglo-Saxon England). This tree stood until a few years ago, when wind finally toppled it.

The mansion was listed on the National Register of Historic Places in 1972. Recent efforts have raised enough money to allow the construction of a new roof and restore a wall that collapsed. The group is now trying to raise money to restore the windows and interior. The "cathedral-like" barns are no longer there, and were probably Dutch style. The society has an annual Winter Harvest Festival fundraiser with good food, reenactors and tours of the mansion and grounds.

While the roots are here, the name Knickerbocker has become pervasive in America. Locally, you may remember the *Knickerbocker News*, or the Knickerbocker (now Pepsi) Arena. In the illustrations of Irving's early editions of his history, Knickerbocker is portrayed wearing loose-fitting breeches, or trousers that end just below the knee. This type of pants was worn in the nineteenth century by males engaged in various athletics, and became known as "knickerbockers." By 1881, the term was shortened to "knickers," and was still common in the 1930s and '40s. Even the New York Knickerbockers ("Knicks") had, as their original logo, a Dutchman (Knickerbocker) dribbling a ball. The name Knickerbocker was later used to identify the first American school of writers, the Knickerbocker Group.

During the October months, "Knick at Night" would once again entertain the "reported" ghosts of the Knickerbockers and their friends haunting the spooky chambers during evening hours.

However, before you visit, be sure to read Irving's *Legend of Sleepy Hollow*. It will put you in the fright frame of mind.

PART III
Natural Wonders

A River Deep in History

The mighty 315-mile Hudson River has had many names: the North River, Manhattes, Rio de Montagne and *Muhhekunnetuk*. In fact, the Hudson is not technically a river for half its length, but rather a fjord, or estuary, of the Atlantic Ocean.

History books claim that "The River of the Steep Hills" was discovered by Giovanni da Verrazzano in 1524 and explored by Hendrick Hudson, who called it the "River of Mountains," in 1609.

Wrong! Considering that both Verrazzano and Hudson encountered a diversity of native people during their visits, they hadn't "discovered" anything. They merely stumbled on a region that was well settled for thousands of years by native people, the Muhhekaneok, or Mohicans.

Writing in his journals, Hudson found that "the river is full of fish" and "the land is the finest for cultivation that I ever in my life set foot upon." Hudson, for the most part, enjoyed his contact and trade, which included oysters, tobacco, currants and many species of fish, including "young salmon and sturgeons."

When the Dutch and later English settled permanently on Mohican lands, visitors to the region often wrote about the beauty of the river, its contents and its shores. Two Dutch missionaries remarked in 1679, "The

North river abounds with fish of all kinds, throughout from the sea to the falls."

When David Pieterzoon de Vries bought Staten Island in 1639, he visited Albany. He found white and blue grapevines along the river, along with swans, geese, pigeons, teal and wild geese. The numerous islands in the river "were covered with chestnuts, plum, hazel nut, and large walnuts."

In 1651, one Dutchman writing to another remarked about the abundance of cod and sturgeon in the river "that the sturgeon above all is in your rivers in such abundance and can be taken in such vast quantities that the Caviar could as well be manufactured there as muscovy." Sturgeon congregated at the base of the Cohoes Falls to propagate, and this was a sight to see, according to witnesses.

Sturgeon certainly was abundant in the Hudson. At one time Albany was called Sturgeonville and sturgeon was called "Albany Beef." Albany's citizens were called "Surgeonites from Sturgeondom."

Sturgeons were four to eight feet long and weighed 100 to 450 pounds—one weighed in at 486 pounds. April to September was harvest time, and about 20 per day were caught, often getting about 2,500 per season. One hundred barrels of oil were extracted also and used for lighting and medicinal uses.

Adrian van der Donk in 1654 called the river "seer visryck," Dutch for "very fish rich." He also wrote, perhaps prophetically, that "his attention was arrested by the Hudson, in which a painter could find rare and beautiful subjects for his brush." The Hudson River School appeared two hundred years later.

Peter Kalm in 1750 wrote, "Sturgeons abound in the Hudson River. We saw them all day long leaping high up into the air, especially in the evening." He goes on to say, "Where the tide stops at the Hudson there being only a small and shallows streams above it. At that place they catch a good many kinds of fish in the river." Kalm continued with his natural history assessment, remarking on the various trees and wild grapevines "on the rising shores of the river, where some asparagus grew wild."

Herring, shad, bass, salmon and other fish were also found in abundance. In 1804, one net yielded forty thousand shad in one day. Fishing was certainly an important industry along the Hudson.

Today, shad, striped bass, herring and sturgeon still spawn in the Hudson, but you don't eat them. Starting in 1947, wastewater discharges containing large quantities of PCBs flowed from two General Electric plants at Hudson Falls and Fort Edward into the waters and sediments of the river next to the plants. From these areas, the PCBs have moved down the entire river system through natural and human-directed causes.

Recreational fishing was banned in the upper Hudson below Hudson Falls between 1976 and 1995. It's currently limited to catch and release only along this section. Fish in other areas of the Hudson are subject to consumption advisories of varying degrees due to PCB contamination.

The short-nosed sturgeon spawns in areas of contaminated sediments located immediately below the dam at Troy. PCB concentrations in fish in the Hudson have historically been detected well above the two ppm tolerance level recommended by the FDA. Since 1983, PCB concentrations in fish in the main trunk of the river have shown little evidence of decline.

Today, the short-nose sturgeon is on the Federal Endangered Species List. What about the river?

Bridge over Hudson Waters

Part of being human is dealing with challenges. One interesting challenge in our history has been how to cross large bodies of water. Recent archaeological evidence suggests that the first people to populate America may have traveled from Polynesia by boat, and not just simply walked across a land connection in the Bering Straits, as previously thought.

Once people arrived, the next challenge was crossing mighty rivers like the Hudson. Today, we laugh at the idea that crossing a river is much of a problem. Our modern technology whizzes us over bridges in seconds. We barely know we are crossing water in some bridge designs! But it wasn't so long ago that crossing the Hudson by bridge at Troy or Albany was a major political battle that took years to accomplish. Troy won. Well, actually, Lansingburgh was first.

A nineteenth-century view of the first Albany Maiden Lane Bridge. *Courtesy of the Albany Public Library.*

The Union Bridge, built in 1804, was the first bridge to span the Hudson, connecting Waterford to Lansingburgh at the site of the present bridge. At a cost of $20,000, it was declared an engineering feat. Large hewn timbers squared by hand axes were pinioned together with large wooden pegs and iron strips welded together. When it burned down in 1909, it was the oldest covered bridge in America. Originally built for trolleys, and toll based, a newer iron bridge with fireproof floors took its place and was toll free.

In 1834, the Rensselaer and Saratoga Railroad spanned Troy to Green Island with a covered wooden bridge. It was the first bridge in Troy and the only bridge between New York City and Waterford. It was the fuel for Troy's largest fire when a spark from an idling train engine ignited the timbers of the bridge in 1862. More than 507 buildings were burned to the ground, taking out most of downtown up to Eighth Street. Remarkably, only five people died.

A second railroad bridge was built to take its place between 1876 and 1884, but made of iron and steel. In 1977, I drove over the bridge an hour before it came crashing down into the River, when a pier from the original bridge gave way.

In 1872, the second Troy bridge was built at the foot of Congress Street at a cost of $350,000. It was the second largest highway bridge in America and was featured in *Scientific American*. It was replaced in 1915–17 by a newer, electrically controlled drawbridge and became toll free. The Department of Transportation had to blow it up in 1971 to replace it with the present span.

In 1880, Cohoes was connected by bridge to Lansingburgh. This bridge burned as well, to be followed by an iron bridge with wooden floors. It burned on March 4, 1920. A temporary hanging footbridge (like the one in *Indiana Jones*) was erected. Old-timers tell me that they used to call it the "Swing," as it rocked back and forth when the winds were blowing. A new, toll-free concrete bridge was built in 1923.

The last historic bridge was the Menands Bridge, built in 1933, connecting South Troy to Menands. The towers have recently been taken down and there are plans to remove it for a new one.

Troy and Albany fought for the first bridge rights. Albany actually proposed building a bridge in January 1814, but was opposed by Troy, Lansingburgh and Waterford. Albany tried again in 1831, '35, '41, '54 and '56. It wasn't until April 9, 1856, that the Hudson River Bridge Company got legislative approval, forty-two years after its first attempt!

On February 22, 1866, Albany's first bridge opened. It was built on twenty-one stone piers and cost $750,000, crossing the river at Livingston

Street. Rebuilt over the years, it went from serving freight trains to both freight and passenger use today. This may be the oldest nineteenth-century bridge of its kind still spanning the Hudson. So, Albany wins the battle in the long run. None of Troy's earliest bridges remain standing.

Today, a little cabin, no larger than an average size bedroom, sits on top of the Albany bridge. George Ford, a thirty-five-year railroad man, swings open the bridge several times a day to let boats through. Manning one of three shifts, George peers at a large wooden board that takes up the northern length of the cabin—from above it he can see a beautiful bird's-eye view of the Hudson. The board is filled with red and yellow monitor lights along an imaginary set of lines representing tracks. Using his thirty-five years of experience, George throws any series of switches that control the direction of the tracks, to make sure that all trains crossing through the Rensselaer Station area stay on course.

George takes his job in stride, as most professionals do. However, it represents one of the last unique (probably disappearing) jobs in America, and one which has been going on at this site for 134 years.

Seven Man-made Wonders of the Capital District

The seven historic jewels of the nineteenth century that are selected here can still be seen. Since there are many to choose from, I solicited the help of historians P. Thomas Carroll, Rachel Bliven and John Wolcott.

Bleecker Reservoir

Bleecker Reservoir was built in 1851 and is the biggest artificial earthwork in the city of Albany. Most water supplies are either dammed lakes, streams or reservoirs dug into the ground. Bleecker is a man-made rectangular structure built of earth above ground. It takes up two city blocks, 157,600 square feet, and when active held 32 million gallons of water in the 880- by 520-foot rectangle that was about 40 feet high.

Water depth was maintained at 15 feet, and distributed to all of Albany residents west of Pearl Street before it was abandoned in 1932. It was converted to a stadium in 1935.

A labor strife ignited when Bleecker was built. Workers toiled for ten hours per day, six days a week for 62½ cents per week. They rioted in 1851, asserting that they had been promised $1 a day.

Cast-Iron Storehouse

Situated on the grounds of the Watervliet Arsenal is a rectangular building with a dimension of 100 by 196 feet, built in 1859. What makes it unique is that the entire building is made from cast iron.

Designed by Daniel Badger's Architectural Iron Works in New York City, this may be the only remaining example of a complete iron building still being used for its original purpose, although it now houses an arsenal museum.

Cast iron for architecture became a booming business after the Civil War and continued until the 1940s. You can still see hundreds of cast-iron storefronts in our area.

Erie Canal

It's hard to deny that the construction of the Erie Canal, which opened in 1825, was a remarkable engineering achievement. Dug by farmers, local people and immigrant labor, toiling fourteen hours a day, they connected Buffalo to Albany with their sweat and labor. They even invented a few tools along the way to do the job better, like stump-pulling devices, for example.

The Erie Canal, when completed, was 425 miles long, 40 feet wide and only 4 feet deep on average. Combine that with several lateral canals and the Champlain Canal, and there were about 1,000 miles of canals in the state.

The Erie Canal opened up New York State for commerce by providing an easy distribution route east–west and north–south. It quickly made New York Harbor the number one port in the country. Cities and industries were born and grew along the canal route.

Cast-iron storehouse at the Watervliet Arsenal. Designed by Daniel Badger's
Architectural Iron Works in New York City, this may be the only remaining example of
a complete iron building still being used for its original purpose, although it now houses
an arsenal museum. *Courtesy of the Library of Congress.*

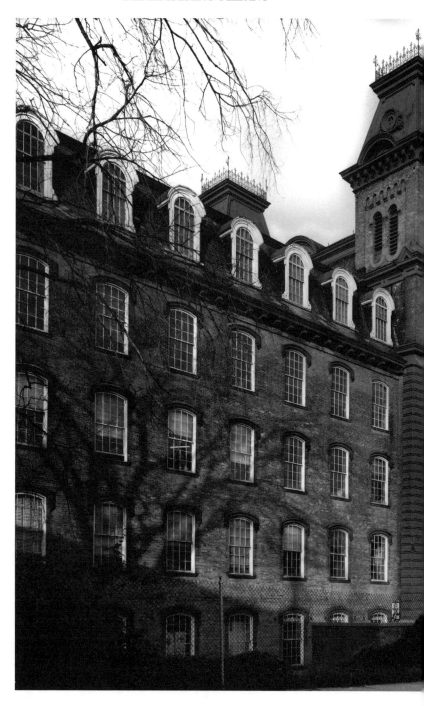

Harmony Mill #3 at Cohoes. It was here that the famous Cohoes mastodon was dug up while the building was under construction in 1866. This skeleton is almost eleven thousand years old. *Courtesy of the Library of Congress.*

There are many examples of engineering achievements related to the canal that you can visit, such as the Rexford Aqueduct, Waterford locks of the Champlain Canal and several examples of the original canal bed and locks throughout the Capital District. This was New York's Thruway of the nineteenth century.

Harmony Hills Complex, Boyden Turbines

Harmony Hills, located near the Cohoes Falls, was known as the largest and most complete cotton manufacturing establishment in the United States from the late 1860s through the 1880s. It was the single largest American producer of cotton fabrics for printed calicoes and fine cotton muslins, which were spun and woven from raw cotton right in the mills.

Inside Mill No. 3, built in 1866–72, are some of the largest vertical turbines in the United States. They took water power and converted it to mechanical power as it turned a system of belts to run various machines. Two of the turbines produced eight hundred horsepower each. In this one mill, thirteen miles of belts powered 2,700 looms and 130,000 spindles, which could produce 100,000 yards of cloth every sixty hours.

The Boyden turbine design was the first to be manufactured in quantity in the United States and became the standard in the textile industry from 1844 to about 1880. The two here were the largest built. This site is now a National Historic Mechanical Engineering Landmark.

Gas Holder House

Located on the northwest corner of Jefferson Street and Fifth Avenue is a large round building that was built in 1873 for one purpose—to store and distribute coal gas throughout the city of Troy. This is one of the few remaining examples of a gas holder house, which once was commonplace in northeastern cities.

The building is actually a brick sheath that surrounded an iron holder with a floating top that went up or down depending on the amount of gas continued within. There were single-, double- and triple-lift type gasholders. The Troy gasholder was a two-lift type. Both sections were about 100 feet around and 22 feet thick. At capacity, it held 330,000 cubic feet of gas moving through pipes of twelve inches.

The building protected the gas holder from the elements and provided a sense of security to nearby residents—this was at a time when gas was used to light homes and businesses.

It was built for the Troy Gas Light Company, which maintained a twenty-seven-year monopoly on gas distribution, eventually merging with several others into the Troy Gas Company. This gas holder went out of service in the 1920s. The gas holder itself was sold in 1930 as scrap. All that remains is the house.

Mohawk and Hudson Railroad

New York's successful Erie Canal had one glitch. Between the Mohawk and Hudson River, you had to navigate through several locks—a forty-mile route—and it took all day. George Featherstonhaugh, from Duanesburgh, decided to build a railroad between the two cities that would cut the time more than in half. He announced the formation of the Mohawk and Hudson Railroad Company on December 28, 1825.

A sixteen-mile route was constructed between Albany and Schenectady through the pine bush. It opened for service August 9, 1831, and was the first steam passenger train in the country running a regular schedule.

The original bed used blocks of stone with a wooden rail capped with iron. The first steam engine, the Dewitt Clinton, pulled modified stagecoaches. The last remaining piece of this roadbed can be seen on Washington Avenue Extension in Albany, but developments in front of it destroy the natural view of the landscape.

Whipple Cast and Wrought-Iron Bowstring Truss Bridges

Squire Whipple, a Union College graduate, designed and patented the design of the iron arch truss, or bowstring truss, in 1841, used in bridge construction. Known as Whipple bridges, they were widely used over the Erie Canal, but when his patent ran out in 1869, the design was copied in every detail by other bridge makers and his patent was infringed. He

Visitors admiring the replica of the Hudson and Mohawk Railroad, Dewitt Clinton, around 1909. *Courtesy of the Efner Research Library.*

was unable to collect. Whipple was the first engineer to analyze correctly the stresses in a bridge truss.

There are three examples of Whipple bridges in our area. One spans the Normans Kill in the village of Normansville, under Delaware Avenue. Another is on the campus of Union, while a third is part of a park in Rexford.

Seven Ancient Wonders of the Capital District

Most people don't have a clue about the earth they walk on or drive over. Folks are always in a hurry, zipping along, trying to get to work or wherever it is they think they need to be in 3.5 seconds. I suppose as long as the land doesn't move suddenly, folks simply don't give it a second thought.

However, for those of you who like to be aware of your surroundings and have a desire to understand the complexities of the world, we have a varied and interesting geological history in the Capital District. It may even startle you to realize that some of the geographic features you think are gneiss to look at, but take for granite every day, actually were formed thousands of miles from here under totally different environmental conditions.

So the next time you're at a loss to find a place to take the in-laws, or friends from out of town, try impressing them with a little field trip to the following—the seven ancient wonders of the Capital District.

Cohoes Falls (City of Cohoes, Albany County)

A European tourist site as early as 1642, it was well known for thousands of years by Native Americans who came down the Mohawk River by boat. Canoeists would disembark up from the falls and carry their boats down around the falls to trade with the Europeans.

Cohoes is said to be Mohawk for "overturned canoe"—aptly named. The falls is 1,140 feet wide and 86 feet high. It was a major tourist attraction until Niagara Falls became a tourist Mecca starting in the 1820s. Its water power supplied several of the nineteenth-century textile mills nearby.

Over the last twelve thousand years, the Cohoes Falls has migrated five kilometers upstream from where the Mohawk meets the Hudson. The best time to view the Cohoes Falls is early spring.

Cohoes Falls.

Above: The Cohoes Falls today. It is the site where the Great Peacemaker, also known as Deganawida, performed his feat of strength, convincing the Mohawk people to become the founders of the Iroquois League of Nations. *Courtesy of Don Rittner.*

Left: The Cohoes Falls, from *Picturesque America* by William Cullen Bryant, 1874. Several paintings and views exist, as this was one of the ancient wonders of America until the Niagara Falls became a tourist attraction. *Courtesy of Don Rittner.*

Heritage on the Hudson

Helderberg Escarpment (Albany County)

Running from Albany to Auburn, the Helderberg Mountains form the northern boundary of the Allegheny Plateau. These Devonian-era rocks of 410 million years ago were laid down in an expanding sea that covered New York State. Known as the Helderberg Group, it consists of layers of limestone that were heavily mined during the nineteenth century and continue to be mined today.

Emma Treadwell Thatcher, the widow of John Thatcher, mayor of Albany, donated the eastern end of the Helderbergs, called Indian Ladder or Thatcher Park, to the state in 1913. It provides one of the most beautiful views of Albany County. You can see the various limestone formations and even some fossils here along the Indian Ladder trail.

On top of the escarpment, on a road leading to Thatcher Park, is a large coral reef formed when the area was south of the equator 350 million years ago.

A view of Thatcher Park and the Helderbergs. *Courtesy of Don Rittner.*

Petrified Sea Gardens and Lester Park (Greenfield Town, Saratoga County)

Visiting the Petrified Sea Gardens is like stepping back to a time about five hundred million years ago. This park is about an acre of exposed cryptozoon stromatolite fossils—colonial blue-green algae that form large concentric formations that have been called "stone cabbage." This huge slab of fossils was once part of an ocean reef that existed when our area was at the edge of a warm tropical sea near the equator. Stromatolites are some of the earliest known forms of life on the planet.

The land is owned by a quarry company and is in constant danger of being destroyed. A nonprofit group, Friends of Petrified Sea Gardens, manages the park and charges a small fee for admittance.

Just up the road is Lester Park, where you can also see stromatolites on the side of the road. This is where James Hall, father of American geology and New York State geologist, first described the genus cryptozoon. Attorney Willard Lester donated Lester Park to the State Museum in 1914.

The Pine Bush (Albany and Schenectady Counties)

The pine bush, or pine barrens, is a large sand delta, originally forty square miles, that was laid down by the ancient Mohawk River emptying into Lake Albany. Lake Albany was a large glacial lake that spanned Lake George to New York City, filling the Hudson Valley. It is the home of the endangered Karner blue Butterfly and hundreds of other rare plants and animals. There are only about twenty pine barrens in the world. The pine bush ranks in the top five in size, but has been reduced to a few thousand acres by human development.

Saratoga Geyser (Saratoga State Park, Saratoga County)

A geyser is a hot spring that periodically erupts, throwing water into the air. Worldwide, there are only a total of seven hundred geysers.

The Albany pine bush. This is a rare inland pine barrens environment and home of the endangered Karner blue butterfly. *Courtesy of Don Rittner.*

In Saratoga State Park there are two hot springs, the Orenda Spring and Geyser Spring. Both can be seen when walking along the creek in the park off Geyser Road. Artesian in formation, the geyser blows its top regularly, and the resulting calcite or carbonate deposits form a huge mound around it. The Orenda Spring has a large flow of carbonate deposit that runs into the creek. The geology of the springs is probably part of the extensive underground springs that run through the Saratoga Fault, some sixty-five miles between Whitehall and Albany. Scientists are not sure how this geyser works. This is the only spouting geyser east of the Mississippi River.

Stark's Knob (Schuylerville, Saratoga County)

About two miles north of Schuylerville, at the north end of the Saratoga Battlefield, is Stark's Knob, also known as the Schuylerville Volcano.

General John Stark had a redoubt (fortification) built on this once dome-shaped volcanic knoll. There he foiled General Burgoyne's attempt to withdraw his troops north during the American Revolution.

Originally thought of as a volcanic dyke, plug or neck when found, it is now known as a pillow basalt (lava) formation that was transported

Kevin, Jack and Chris at the geyser in Saratoga. The Saratoga State Park has the only active spouting geysers east of the Mississippi River in the United States. This is called the Island Spouter by locals, and it sends a narrow plume of water ten to fifteen feet (three to five meters) into the air. It first emerged in the early 1900s. *Courtesy of Don Rittner.*

probably by the Taconic thrust (mountain-building event) four million years ago. The rock all around the basalt is limestone, so it was most likely a deep warm sea when the lava oozed from the interior of the earth.

The knob was mined for road gravel for a while. It is now owned by the New York State Museum and may be adopted by a local private school for safekeeping and cleanup.

Underground Caverns (Albany and Schoharie Counties)

Underneath the Capital District region lie miles of subterranean caves filled with stalagmites (down) and stalactites (up), flowstone, underground streams and unique formations, all carved out of limestone from flowing underground waters. It took millions of years to carve out these caves. Moreover, it takes one hundred years to create one cubic centimeter of a stalagmite.

The most famous cave in our area is Howe Caverns (www.howecaverns.com) in Howe Caverns, New York, just west of Albany. Howe Caverns is 156 feet below the surface and was discovered in the 1770s. It's believed to have started forming about six million years ago. A tour of the cave tops off with a quarter-mile boat ride on a subterranean lake, which is 2 to 8 feet deep.

In the immediate Capital District, there are many caves you can visit that are well known to the spelunker (cave explorer), including Gage, Bensons, McFails, Knox, Schoharie, Caboose and Clarksville caves.

John Cook was New York's first caver. He was commissioned in the summer of 1906 by the New York State Science Service to explore and report on the caves of Schoharie and Albany Counties.

I used to explore the South Bethlehem cave, which is now closed (quarry blasts made it dangerous). You should never go caving alone—only with experienced spelunkers.

Visit the Spelunking News website (www.topix.com/hobbies/spelunking) to learn more about cave exploring and gaining access.

Diamond Rock Losing Its Luster?

Just east of Lansingburgh and overlooking it is a rise of rock outcrop more than three hundred feet above sea level. Known as Diamond Rock, this stone outcrop is one of the Capital District's most famous natural landmarks. Various geological reports list quartzite, limestone, sandstone and shale as the ingredients, but on a sunny day, Diamond Rock sparkles like diamond from the imbedded quartz crystals found in veins throughout the stone monument.

Standing on top of this summit, one can see the confluence of the Hudson and Mohawk Rivers and more than one hundred miles up and down the Hudson Valley, a view that includes the Catskill Mountains on the south and the Adirondacks on the north. This view is so beautiful that historian John Wolcott told me that the well-to-do Albany trader John Sanders, who owned much of the land that is now Lansingburgh in the seventeenth century, made it a point to take the missionary travelers Dankers and Sluyter on top for a visit in 1679–80.

The "Legend of Diamond Rock" or "The Old Indian's Story of Moneta" legend was told to Nathanial Sylvester and published in 1877. The "diamonds" are really Herkimer diamonds—double-faced quartz crystals. *Courtesy of Don Rittner.*

Heritage on the Hudson

For hundreds of years, local inhabitants and visitors from around the world enjoyed picnics or sightseeing on Diamond Rock. Even gypsy families called it home once in a while. Fireworks were set off there during celebrations like those celebrating Troy Week in 1908.

But today, Diamond Rock is private property for the most part, with housing and commercial developments sprinkled on top, and it is no longer the haven for those who want to commune with nature. Sadly, it is one more example of the chipping away at the features that made Troy so different from the rest of the world—both in terms of natural and human history.

You see, there is a great Indian legend about Diamond Rock and how those "diamonds" (Herkimer diamonds—really double-faced quartz crystals) were formed. It is called the "Legend of Diamond Rock" or "The Old Indian's Story of Moneta." This legend was told to Nathanial Sylvester and published in 1877.

The story goes that a Mohican village covered the flood plain on the east side of the Hudson just opposite the mouth of the Mohawk (probably near Freihofers) and was led by a chief named Hohadora. The chief lived there with his wife, Moneta, and two sons, Onosqua and Taendara.

Onosqua was captured in the north and saved from torture by being adopted by an Adirondack Indian woman who had lost her own son at battle, and Hohadora made several attempts to recapture his son, all failing.

On his deathbed, Hohadora instructed his other son, Taendara, to recover Onosqua alive, or his remains, and bury him next to his father and mother. The village members would take care of Moneta during his absence.

Each night, Moneta would start a fire on top of Diamond Rock so that Taendara would see the light and find his way home. Each night for the next twenty years she sat by the fire crying, her tears falling around her, waiting for her sons to return.

Finally, Taendara, carrying his brother's bones, climbed the summit to reunite with his now aged mother, and as they embraced they were struck by lightning. The next morning when the Indian villagers visited the site, the bones of Onosqua lay on the ground, but Moneta and Taendara were gone. The bare ground sparkled with Moneta's tears—twenty years' worth—all of which were turned into diamonds by the force of the lightning.

Diamond Rock, like Moneta and Taendara, is gone, at least in the public sense of things. On top of Diamond Rock are developments like Terrace at High Pointe, complete with roadways like Ridge Circle, Outlook Court, Woods Path and Diamond Rock Circle. How quaint! Why is it that developers like to name their roads after the area they destroy? Was an archaeological survey conducted there before approval?

Another question. How does an area that was in the public use for hundreds, no, thousands of years become private property? You can't park your car unless you live there. There are signs that say "High Pointe Residents Only" and "Unauthorized Vehicles Towed Away."

On the west side of Diamond Rock, along Gurley Avenue, you can find the Diamond Ridge, Gracious Retirement Living complex and Diamond Rock Terrace, Senior Apartments. Opening soon is the Lansingburgh Store-It, a self-storage facility.

One city official told historian Wolcott that Diamond Rock was the last place in Troy where people with money could live comfortably, and developing there was considered "progress." Sorry, but I differ on that assessment. Building houses is for a place to live and is no different than a deer bedding in the woods, or a woodchuck burrowing a tunnel. That isn't "progress."

Progress is humanity learning to live in harmony with itself and having respect and stewardship for the land. Obviously, we have a way to go yet.

I even bet that Moneta is still weeping, but this time it's over the destruction of one of Troy's ancient natural wonders.

A "Clear" Choice

One of my favorite local places is the Helderberg Escarpment in Albany County. As a young boy, I always admired the view of this

Waterfalls at Thatcher Park. The Helderberg Escarpment is the northeastern extent of the Allegheny Plateau, with its juncture with the interior lowlands and the Hudson Valley rising more than one thousand feet above the surrounding area. *Courtesy of Don Rittner.*

geological formation, as it symbolized to me the backdrop of the city of Albany when viewed from Prospect Park. Only later, as a college student, did I learn about the richness of the natural and human history that it contains.

When you admire the escarpment, you're actually admiring events that took place over one billion years ago, when New York was part of a supercontinent called Rodinia located near the South Pole.

Running from Albany to Auburn, the Helderberg Mountains form the northern boundary of the Allegheny Plateau. Known as the Helderberg Group, it consists of layers of limestone and other rock. Rising some two thousand feet above sea level, we know the top of this area as the "escarpment" or "embattlement," and simply as Thatcher Park or Indian Ladder.

Emma Treadwell Thatcher, the widow of Albany mayor John Thatcher, donated the escarpment to New York State in 1913. Recently, more acres have been added, but as I will point out shortly, the new acquisitions came up short of preserving one of the most significant parts of the ridge.

While the Dutch settlers in the area viewed the escarpment like the walls of a fort (hence the name embattlements) and probably had a name for the mountain, though now lost in history, the German settlers gave it the present name, Helderberg, which means "clear mountain." The Palatine Germans, on their way to Schoharie County, named the mountains in 1710. On most days, it certainly lives up to its name.

From a scientific viewpoint, it's a gold mine. Several formations of rock laid down over the last millions of years give the escarpment a "layered" look, a fairly continuous sequence of Late Ordovician to Middle Devonian fossiliferous, marine limestone that existed from 408 to 360 million years ago. Among these layers (fifteen identified) are embedded thousands of mostly marine fossils from bryozoans, corals, brachiopods, bivalves, gastropods, cephalopods, tentaculites and trilobites.

While we know Troy is the birthplace of American geology with Amos Eaton and RPI, the escarpment must be viewed as preschool, as John Gebhard Sr. and Jr., began exploring and describing some of the earliest American invertebrate fossils from the area in the 1820s. Later, the father of American paleontology, Albany's James Hall, by himself used the area to establish North American equivalents for all European described stages of the Devonian era. The Devonian era saw many explosive radiations of species but also mass extinctions during the end of the era. It is also known as the age of fishes, and some fish remains have been found in the Helderberg Group as well.

Parts of the rocks were also known in historic times for their natural gas production, and the thicker beds have been tapped for their abundance of methane. Old gas drills have been found occasionally, and residents of the area do find natural gas in their drinking water.

Helderberg bluestone was also used as building stone and early gravestones, and you can find them with their hand-carved engraved epitaphs throughout the area. Many abandoned quarries dot the landscape.

Of course, historians know the Helderberg area, in particular the town of Berne, as the scene for the famous anti-rent wars of the pre–Civil War era, when farmers rebelled over paying rents to the vestiges of the patroon land system that started in the seventeenth century. This led to a series of armed clashes between the civil authorities and persons occupying land on which rent was owed. The farmers were dressed in calico and Indian garb, and were called "Calico Indians" so they wouldn't be recognized. There was one episode when the Albany sheriff was tarred and feathered by the anti-renters.

However, one of the most unusual formations on the ridge is a large coral reef, composed of honeycomb coral, on Ketcham Road, formed when the area was about three degrees south of the equator, 350 million years ago, while in tropical waters. Blacksmith Martin Milner of Voorheesville owns the reef, and parts of it were mined years ago. Recent additions to the park stop right at Milner's property line.

Why the state did not purchase this world-famous coral reef is beyond me. Martin will certainly sell it, he tells me, and perhaps now that we call attention to it, New York State will purchase it in the near future.

After all, you don't find a 350-million-year-old coral reef at two thousand feet above sea level every day!

History of the Blues

In the fall of 1974, entomologists Bob Dirig, John Cryan and I were sitting in Room 10 in the M&M motel in Guilderland. Our task was to find a mascot for the Pine Bush Preservation Project, an endeavor I began to help save the pine bush, a unique and endangered wilderness between Albany and Schenectady. I knew then that we needed to have something that the public could rally around, and that among the thousands of plants and animals that called the pine bush home, there had to be one that could symbolize why the area should be saved.

After going through a litany of little animals, including moths, beetles and dragonflies, we agreed on the Karner blue Butterfly (*Lycaeides melissa samuelis*). This little blue butterfly was not only endangered, being restricted to living in pine barrens–type environments such as the pine bush, but it also had a bit of interesting folklore. Bob and John had been studying the biology of the butterfly for over a year and had built up quite a remarkable knowledge base on this little one-inch-wide work of nature.

The KB had been given its name by novelist Vladimir Nabokov, better known for works like *Lolita*. Before his fame as a fiction writer, he was a first-class entomologist and was studying the whole family of blues during the '30s and '40s. Nabokov gave the butterfly, previously known as Scudder's Blue, the name "Karner" after the little railroad station in the pine bush by that name. This is where Nabokov disembarked in search of his specimens when they were on the wing. The pine bush is the type locality of the KB, and the KB is the type specimen. For scientists, it means that this is the home base and the population that all future research on the butterfly has to be based on. Nabokov took to his little blue personally and even featured it in one of his novels (*Pnin*). In a letter to Dirig, he remembered the butterfly's home as a "flowery and sandy little paradise."

After a talk I gave at the annual Wildlife Society meeting in 1974, a DEC biologist and department head approached me and asked what should be done to save the butterfly. I suggested making it the official endangered insect of New York State. He put into action the preparation of the papers and legislative support to make it happen. It became the first insect to be designated as officially endangered in New York State, and that act helped save hundreds of acres of pine bush, not to mention give the butterfly a few more years of longevity.

In 1978, we nominated the butterfly as a federally threatened species, but Mayor Erastus Corning, then head of the Albany political machine, scuttled it. He felt it would have stopped all future development in the pine bush—which was our intent, of course. It would take twenty more years—and now a dwindling population of Karner blues—to finally have it listed as endangered on the federal level. It's probably too late now for the butterfly's long-term survival.

While the KB became the rallying cry for saving the pine bush (some protesters even wore KB wings at anti-development hearings), the butterfly was dwindling around all its population centers, and even became extinct in Massachusetts.

When I used to give tours to children's groups, there were literally thousands of KBs flying during a day and often one would land on my finger and take the entire tour with the kids, duly impressing even the most ardent bug hater. Today, if you see one KB you feel lucky.

There are around three thousand acres of pine bush preserved now, but the KB is not doing well. Populations have suffered throughout its range over the years due to habitat destruction and other factors. It has not deterred folks from promoting the butterfly, however.

Ohio artist and naturalist Gretchen Rettig, who first worked in horticulture, turned to art via oil, acrylic and photography, including digital, and has a great rendering of an "angel" with Karner blue wings at www.elfwood.com/~grettig/Karner_Blue_Lady_Lycaeides_melissa_samuelis_Angel.2775416.html.

Wisconsin artist Barb Pelowski expresses herself through enamels and patchwork. She has produced some dazzling representations of the Karner blue in pin and pendant form. Her artwork can be seen at www.barbpel.com.

Janet and Kevin Oberembt from Indiana operate Curio Cabinet Antiques on the web and offer miniature ceramic shoe collections. They sell a beautiful Karner blue high heel miniature for twenty dollars at www.dealersdirect.com/Dealer/Oberembt/Antiques/rightshoe.html.

Finally, Sissy Provost, a young woman from Schenectady, wants one hundred butterflies tattooed on her body. Last week she took a postcard of the Karner blue and had it tattooed on her neck for all to enjoy.

Fortunately, the Karner blue blues will never be sung.

A Sense of Place

When one views nineteenth-century illustrations of Albany and Troy, it's almost always a viewpoint from the Hudson River. We are beginning the process of reclaiming our mighty Hudson, but I would like to put out a warning not to rush so fast.

Those visions of the cities from the river offered the river cruiser a familiar site when he or she reached our ports. If the destination was Albany, the sight of the original capitol building; St. Peter's and Second Baptist Churches, along with other church spires; or grandiose city, state and Stanwix Halls all told you that home was near. Likewise, viewers of Troy saw the "Towers of Troy" (old Troy Seminary, where the RPI library now sits), Mount Ida, collar and cuff factories and other familiar scenes.

Amazingly, you could also see each city in its entirety as the buildings and streets draped the flood plain and river benches carpeting the land while rising to higher lands to the east or west. Each homecomer or visitor could feel a sense of place.

The beauty of the Hudson even spawned its own art school, and the Hudson River School paintings that were born as a result are held in the highest regard in the art world today.

If, or should I say, when we take back the river, we should ensure that there still is that sense of place, but there are threats in the wind that could make our region look like any other—the threat of allowing the wrong kind of river development could destroy our chance for rejuvenation.

Case in point: we already know how Albany turned its back on the river after it let the DOT (Department of Transgressions) take the riverfront for I-787 during the 1970s. Only in recent times has the city tried to bridge its citizens back to the river.

Heritage on the Hudson

There is no view of nineteenth-century downtown Watervliet along the river. In fact, there is no downtown Watervliet. It was demolished and taken up for I-787.

Somehow, a new apartment complex was approved and crammed on the old Troy landfill on Center Island, and folks on the Troy side enjoying a good brew or food at the Troy Pub must view apartment dwellers hanging out their balconies perched very close to the island's cliffs. I predict that one of those buildings slides down into the river.

The city of Troy wants to put a new truck route from downtown to South Troy, which baffles me. Why not let heavy trucks use the existing I-787 from the Watervliet side and go over the Menands Bridge into industrial South Troy? This prevents the obvious catastrophe it would cause by having trucks barreling down the riverfront of Troy. After all, there is a plan on the table to make the entire riverfront a greenway. A truck route would certainly impact that.

I recently saw a plan that had twenty-story apartment buildings lining Troy's riverfront. Ouch! How would one even know there is a city behind them?

Our friends in Rensselaer are fighting to keep their riverfront from becoming a smokestack and recycling plant by fighting off Besicorp. It seems logical to clean that parcel up as close to pure as possible and use it to develop a brand-new downtown Rensselaer with shops, homes and businesses, and of course a green riverfront.

Doing anything else would create an ugly stretch of river from Albany to Troy and would devastate any plans of revitalizing the river. A friend of mine who belongs to an ice-racing group farther south put it bluntly to me recently. He told me that they would never come to Albany because of its ugly concrete riverfront and spaghetti highway.

We have a rare opportunity to get back to the Hudson, to engage our senses like those before us who enjoyed the river for thousands of years. With the upcoming Troy Boat and Maritime Center, and the creation of a new Trojan boat-building industry, the river future in Troy looks good.

We can make the Hudson between Albany and Waterford worth its weight in gold, but we must plan carefully, or lose it once more to the clutches of unforgiving industry and greed.

J.W. Barber. del.

S.E. VIEW OF ALBANY,

The City and State Halls each surmounted with a dome, are seen towe *entrance of the Erie Canal is seen on the*

An 1845 view of Albany from Rensselaer. City hall and state hall (with domes) can be seen, along with many warehouses along the riverfront. *Courtesy of the Albany Public Library.*

Sherman & Smith. sc. N.Y.

GREENBUSH FERRY.

e other buildings on the hill on which Albany is mostly built. The
th or Greenbush Ferry Landing. on the left .

Or, as Trojan Ms. A.H. Mosher stated in 1846:

Who loveth not our river?
With its bright and silver wave,
That glides so noiselessly along
To find its ocean grave.
Year after year, it hath wound its way,
And 'tis passing now, as 'twas yesterday.

Shoring Up Our Roots

Over four hundred years ago, Peyhaunet, Aepjen, Amenhamit, Wanapet and their families, all members of the Mohican nation, lived along the banks and flood plain of the *Muhhekunnetuk*. While their children played around the small villages of circular wooden homes, their fathers hunted in the forests. Their mothers gathered nuts and berries along the banks of the river in the land that we now call Troy.

Where currently sits Congress, Ferry, State and River Streets once stood a forest of red spruce, oak, pine, maple and birch trees. This forest was filled with white-tailed deer, moose, beaver, otter, bobcat, mink, wild turkey and other animals that served as food, and also as symbols of family relationships. The forests were broken in places with open cultivated fields that grew corn, beans and squash.

Along the banks and islands of the river grew white and blue grapes, chestnuts, plum, hazelnut and large walnuts, with flocks of swans, geese, pigeons, teal and wild geese making their homes there as well. The river itself teemed with four-hundred-pound sturgeons and millions of herring, shad, bass and salmon, not to mention tons of shellfish.

This was the scene encountered when Henry Hudson first visited our region in 1609.

Is it any wonder that Adrian van der Donk wrote in 1654 that his "attention was arrested by the Hudson, in which a painter could find rare and beautiful subjects for his brush"? He was way ahead of his time, as the Hudson River School of painting didn't appear until 1835, some 181 years later.

No matter what you call it—the North River, Manhattes, Mauritius, Rio de Montaigne, Rio San Antonio or *Muhhekunnetuk*—today's Hudson River is the artery that nourished our region for thousands of years.

Even as the Mohicans shared their land with the Dutch, English and other nationalities, and eventually were replaced by these European transplants, the Hudson River remained the focal point for trade, transportation and life-sustaining food.

River transportation continued to be the primary way to move people and goods—even with the advent or roads, turnpikes and trains—right up to the 1960s. The millions of pounds of fish taken from the river fed many a palate. Millions of mass-produced products found their markets as they were carried down the river and shipped farther to ports around the world. Writers and artists immortalized the river for centuries, and the Hudson drew millions of people to it annually.

But then something drastic happened. We turned our back on our river. We saw it as a place to dump our man-made garbage and toxic wastes. We cut ourselves off from the river by building highways along its banks. We stopped eating the fish that was now full of contaminants. Many started seeing the river only as an obstacle to cross.

Fortunately, there were those who began to alert us of what we were doing to the river more than thirty years ago. Environmental laws were passed and enforced during the 1970s. People like folk singer Pete Seeger and the crew of the sloop *Clearwater* sailed up and down the river during the '80s speaking out for the river. Those who turned their backs to the river realized what a serious mistake they made and scrambled to reverse their errors.

In recent years, cities like Albany have spent millions of dollars to try and bridge the river back to its people. In nearby Troy, we are only beginning to realize what a treasure we still have—several miles of riverfront waiting to be rediscovered.

Can it be done? Anthropologist Margaret Mead said it best: "Never doubt that a handful of committed people can change the world. Indeed, it is the only thing that ever has."

PART IV

Ingenuity

History on a Roll

Sometimes I amaze myself on what I find while doing research. There are many things we take for granted; yet we must realize that someone has to invent those items we regularly use, even though we really never think or talk about them. One of those items is toilet paper. Someone had to invent it, right? The average American uses 57 sheets of toilet paper a day, or more than 20,805 sheets a year, to create this $2.4 billion industry. That's a lot of sheet.

It seems like this little necessity has absorbed our interest for ages. Chinese emperors ordered toilet paper in two- by three-foot sheets as early as AD 1391; the Bureau of Imperial Supplies produced 720,000 sheets of toilet paper a year. In America, New York's Joseph C. Gayetty manufactured the first packaged pre-moistened sheets of toilet paper in 1857, which he called "therapeutic paper." Packs of 500 sheets were sold for fifty cents. He was so proud that his name was imprinted on each sheet (no jokes please). He advertised it as "The Greatest Necessity of the Age! GAYETTY'S Medicated Paper, FOR THE WATER-CLOSET." It contained aloe, but acceptance by the public was neither smooth nor immediate. Not everyone used the specially made toilet paper, and alternatives competed cheek to cheek.

Many outhouses conveniently set aside baskets of leaves or mussel shells; in rural areas, the soft, porous pages of the Sears-Roebuck Catalog were ideal. In fact, when Sears went to color-coated, shiny paper, it received tons of complaints. Other innovative tools included discarded sheep wool, sponges, newsprint—you get the picture.

Manufacturers were reluctant to place their names on their products, nor was it a discussion topic at parties. People were discreet, as evident from a fan, known in the vernacular as "Madam's Double Utility Fan," found in a house dated 1785. It had a hidden compartment in the handle that contained 150 sheets of toilet paper cut to conform to the shape of the fan.

Marketing toilet paper on a roll is usually credited to the Scott Paper Company in Philadelphia, founded by two brothers, E. Irvin and Clarence Scott, in 1879, and originally from Saratoga. The British Perforated Paper Company also sold toilet paper in 1880, but not on a roll. Instead, its rolled paper catered to barbers, who ripped off pieces to mop up razors. Scott Company was so embarrassed by its toilet paper that it instead used the brand name Waldorf, starting in 1902.

Of course, I wouldn't be writing this piece unless I was going to unroll a local connection, right?

In 1871, the first U.S. patent for perforated wrapping paper was awarded to Seth Wheeler of Albany. The paper was wound into rolls and could easily be torn off at the perforations. Toilet paper was already manufactured in rolls; now only the step of perforation was needed in the production, either with a row of holes or short cuts.

Wheeler was born in Chatham on May 18, 1838, attended Albany Academy and worked at his father's Wheeler, Melick & Co., one of the most important makers of agricultural implements. In 1871, he invented his perforated wrapping machine that also printed on each sheet as it left the roll. In 1874, he created the Rolled Wrapping Paper Company at 318 Broadway in Albany, but the company couldn't turn a profit, and in 1877, he reorganized into the Albany Perforated Wrapping Paper (APWP) Company and began manufacturing his "Medicated Toilet Paper." In short, the toilet paper used today was an Albany, New York invention.

Flush with success, the Charmin Wheeler did well and had over one hundred patents. Wheeler also served as president of the Wheeler Heat and Power Company, was vice-president of the Cheney Piano Action Company of Castleton and was president of the Albany County Savings Bank and director of the New York State bank. On April 3, 1860, he married Elizabeth Boyd, with whom he had three sons and two daughters. His sons worked with him in the paper company. APWP had offices in New York, Chicago, Boston, San Francisco, London, Paris, Berlin and Cologne. It owned over 100,000 acres in Nova Scotia.

If you think that I'm implying that this subject is frivolous, let me remind you of the 1973 toilet paper shortage scare. Johnny Carson cracked a joke about the United States facing an acute shortage of toilet paper. The next day, viewers ran out to stores, bought every roll in sight and began hoarding them. Carson apologized the following day for causing the scare and retracted his quote, but people still hoarded their rolls. Let's face it; the thought of not having any two-ply is enough to scare the wits out of even the brawniest tough guy.

A "Chip" Off the Old Block

There's been a great deal of ink about Sematech, the international consortium of computer chip makers wanting to turn Albany into a major research hub. Sematech represents IBM, Intel, Motorola, HP, Texas Instruments, AMD, Philips and others, and will spend $193 million, while the state will supply the remaining $210 million. What's all the fuss? The Capital District has been a cutting-edge research center for years.

Isn't this the same region where Thomas Edison and Charles Steinmetz created an electric industry (GE) in Schenectady that "lit up the world" in 1892? Isn't it where technological innovation allowed American Locomotive (ALCO) to produce seventy-five thousand train engines from early steam to electric, with many of them still hauling around the world? It is the same GE where Irving Langmuir, Vince Schaefer and

The Dudley Observatory, chartered in 1852, is the oldest independent organization in the country supporting research and education in astronomy and the history of astronomy. *Courtesy of John Wolcott.*

Bernie Vonnegut began Project Cirrus in the 1940s, and where Schaefer and Vonnegut invented cloud seeding for the first time while flying over Schenectady. Langmuir went on to win the Nobel Prize in 1932 for his studies on surface chemistry. Vince founded Albany's Atmospheric Sciences Research Center, along with Vonnegut and others. ASRC is a leading research lab in atmospheric sciences to this day.

GE's Ivar Giaever won the Nobel Prize in physics for his discoveries regarding tunneling phenomena in solids in 1973. He's been at RPI since 1988. Of course, RPI and its graduates have always produced innovation. The first science school in the country was also the birthplace of American geology. Many of RPI's graduates made important contributions, such as Eben Horsford (1818–1893), who invented baking soda, or Leffert L. Buck (1837–1909), who built the longest and the highest bridges in the world at the time. You wear

Heritage on the Hudson

Sanford Cluett's (1874–1968) inventions—sanforizing of shirts—or easily carry things thanks to his process that makes paper bags strong. He held over two hundred patents. William Gurley (1821–1887) made engineering and surveyor products that are still envied—and used—all around the world. John L. Riddell (1807–1865) invented the binocular microscope and magnifying glass.

One of the first American scientific observatories, Albany's Dudley Observatory (1852), produced a number of early discoveries and still operates out of Schenectady as an education center. Albany's William Bell Wait invented the New York Point System of Writing for the Blind in the 1870s. Joseph Henry, while teaching at the Albany Academy, discovered mutual electromagnetic induction—the production of an electric current from a magnetic field—and electromagnetic self-induction. Henry constructed some of the most powerful electromagnets of his time, an oar separator, a prototype telegraph and the first electric motor. He also is given credit for encouraging Alexander Graham Bell's invention of the telephone and creating the first series of weather observers in America. Thomas Elkins, an African American, patented an improved refrigerator design in 1879. It also chilled human corpses. He wasn't from Albany, but Glenn Curtis used Albany as the base to make the long-distance flying record from Albany to New York City in 1910.

Troy's John F. Winslow (1810–1892) and Alexander Holley (1832–1882), also RPI grads, introduced into America the Bessemer steel-making process in South Troy during the nineteenth century, which revolutionized the iron industry. This was after Winslow's state-of-the-art Albany Iron Works rolled the protective plates for the USS *Monitor* in a record thirty days. It was Henry Burden whose inventive genius allowed his company to make one horseshoe a second, not only becoming the leading manufacturer of horseshoes but also one of the largest iron companies in America. Philo Penfield Stewart, inventor of the ultimate cooking stove and the Fuller & Warren Company, made innovative heating stoves to keep people warm around the world, and of course the perfection in bell making in Troy by Hanks, Meneely, Jones and Hitchcock allowed Troy to become the bell-making capital of the world. George M. Phelps (1820–1895) was a pioneer in communication technology and made great contributions in early telegraphy from making keys and telegraph printers, and he was Western Union's lead inventor. P. Thomas Carroll of the Hudson Mohawk Industrial Gateway has rightfully proclaimed Troy as the "Silicon Valley of the Nineteenth Century." Smithsonian historians have called Troy the "Birthplace of the American Industrial Revolution."

During the early period of this country's development, between 1790 and 1850, more than four hundred patents were issued to Capital District inventors on a whole range of innovations. Instead of calling our area "Tech Valley," I think it's more appropriate to call it "Innovation Valley." You see folks, innovation is nothing new to our area. I think the real question is why did it take Sematech so long to realize that?

The Case of the Glass Toe

Cinderella may have been found by her prince with a glass slipper, but the Albany Institute of History and Art can do one better: it has a three-thousand-year-old priestess with a glass toe! She was featured in a special program on the Learning Channel called *The Ancient ER*. It's a good example of how modern technology can aid in historical research.

The mummies at the institute have always been a favorite of mine. They were purchased for the institute in 1908 from the Cairo Museum by an Albany businessman and have been there ever since. Since I was about eight years old, I have visited their resting place and marveled at the exhibit, which today includes more than forty objects along with the two mummies. One mummy is totally wrapped and the other is partially unwrapped and belongs to Ankhefenmut, a priest in the Temple of Mut at Karnak in Thebes during the twenty-first dynasty (circa 1095–945 BC), who is believed to have died in 966. He was between fifty-five and sixty-five years old.

The unwrapped mummy was also believed to be a priest all these years, until Dr. William Wagle, an Albany neuroradiologist, used X-ray, computed tomography (CT) and three-dimensional CT (3D CT) to virtually "unwrap" the mummy. He found a few surprises.

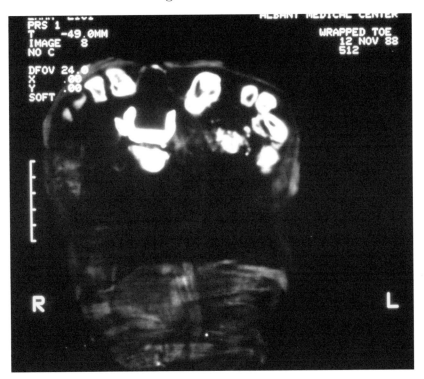

The mummy with the glass toe. Using modern technology, Dr. Wagle was able to discover that the mummy, a female, had a glass toe, which made the body complete so that it could enter the afterlife. *Courtesy of Dr. William Wagle.*

The unwrapped mummy turned out to be a woman of about forty-five to fifty years old, and based on the fact that she came from the same site as the other, is believed to be a priestess. No name is attributed to her since her coffin top never made it to America. Dr. Wagle's work unveiled that inside the mummies were a number of wrapped bundles. This is a change in the mummification practice that occurred during the twenty-first dynasty. The internal organs, which for centuries were put in canopic jars, were now wrapped instead and stuffed back inside the body. Still, the customs related to canopic equipment were so strong that jars remained part of the funerary equipment for the wealthy, but were left empty, or were solid during this period. This change in practice helps date the mummies.

But that wasn't the most surprising thing found. Dr. Wagle noticed that on the big toe of the mummy's right foot was attached a two-part prosthesis—basically an artificial toe. The density of the material revealed a distal hollow piece (-600 Hounsfield CT units) that fits exactly into a dense proximal socket (+1368 units) that may be made of ceramic, ivory or some other high-density non-metallic material. Dr. Wagle believes that it may not have been a functional toe but rather attached to make her "whole," as was the custom of the time to make it to the hereafter. The ER show revealed another artificial toe from a one-thousand-year-old mummy that was discovered later that did show a wear pattern and may have been actually used. Nevertheless, Dr. Wagle's discoveries were the first to reveal this ancient Egyptian medical marvel.

The institute also revealed a new discovery last week along with the promotion of the Learning Channel piece: the mummified "cat," which it has had for more than fifty years, turns out to be a dog, according to the same CT and radiograph techniques that Dr. Wagle used more than ten years ago. Dubbed "Cat-Dog" (your kids will get it!), it is not as unusual as one would think, since cat mummies were common after Bastet, the cat goddess, rose to popularity during the Egyptian Late Period (712–332 BC), but it was equally popular to fake animal mummies that were used at offerings. These mummies were often faked and sold to tourists, both in antiquity and even more recently. The fake mummies were often composed of cloth, feathers, odd bones, brick or pottery or merely some rags, and were wrapped and sold to unsuspecting pilgrims as offerings. Similar substitutions have also been found in hawk mummies from the sacred animal necropolis at Saqqara. Crocodile mummies faked with reeds and bones have also been found.

If you haven't been in the newly redesigned and expanded Albany Institute of History and Art, I suggest you make a visit soon, especially to the Ancient Egypt Gallery. The institute is one of Albany's prize cultural centers and has been a regional icon since 1791, making it one of the oldest institutions of its kind in America.

Their Heads Were in the Clouds

Mark Twain once said, "A great deal has been said about the weather, but very little has been done about it." I attempt to dispel that myth in my reference book, *A to Z Scientists in Weather & Climate*, part of the Facts on File, Inc. Notable Scientists Series.

Thousands of people have been trying to study and predict the weather since Aristotle wrote his *Metereologica* over two thousand years ago. We probably would be way ahead of today's knowledge if Aristotle never wrote that treatment. He was so revered that it didn't matter that most of his conclusions were not scientifically accurate. Scientists used it as gospel, and it wasn't until the sixteenth century and beyond, with the invention of instruments like the thermometer (Galileo), barometer (Torricelli) and hygrometer (De Luc), that empirical data finally was used for making observations and conclusions.

Vincent Schaefer and Bernie Vonnegut, inventors of cloud seeding. *Courtesy of Roger Chang.*

Atmospheric scientist Roger Chang made three important discoveries using a single drop of water. *Courtesy of Roger Chang.*

Heritage on the Hudson

In the two millennia that followed, thousands of men—and, in the twentieth century, women—made great strides in understanding weather and climate. Would you be surprised if I told you that several major discoveries were made by people locally? While I feature a little more than one hundred of the most interesting in my book, seven of them are from our region: Duncan Blanchard, Roger J. Cheng, Joseph Henry, Irving Langmuir, Vincent Schaefer, Maribeth Stolzenburg and Bernard Vonnegut.

Four of the seven—Duncan Blanchard, Irving Langmuir, Vincent Schaefer and Bernard Vonnegut—were part of the famous 1940s "Project Cirrus." Langmuir headed this military project at GE's research and development labs in Schenectady. The other three worked for Langmuir and became part of a team that not only invented cloud seeding but also went on to form the world-renowned Atmospheric Research Science Center (ARSC) based at the University at Albany. However, each scientist made his own contributions to weather and climate.

Blanchard made several important discoveries dealing with electrical charges in the sea and atmosphere and also discovered that when volcanoes erupt through the surface of the sea, the emitting cloud contains droplets of seawater and fragments of lava ash that carry a positive charge. This helps shed light on the origin of lightning strokes from volcanoes when molten lava strikes seawater. His recent book, *The Snowflake Man*, is a biography of Wilson Bentley, the nearby Vermont farmer who was the first to photograph snowflakes.

Vincent Schaefer was a high school dropout and amateur archaeologist who was handy with tools and knew how to design an experiment to solve problems. He worked for Langmuir as a toolmaker but also invented a way to cloud seeds—the first to do so. Schaefer discovered super-cooled water droplets, and that knowledge helped him create his famous cold box (GE brand, naturally), where he produced ice crystals that led to the first cloud seeding in 1946. His colleague, Bernard Vonnegut, brother of writer Kurt Vonnegut, the following day used silver iodide as an effective seeding agent in Schaefer's experiment.

Roger Cheng, who was Schaefer's right-hand man and ran the lab when Schaefer organized ARSC, went on to discover three major findings in cloud physics, marine aerosols and environmental science, all from studying a single drop of water. His beautiful photomicrographs have been on the cover of leading scientific journals.

Joseph Henry, who started his career as an actor, became a teacher at the Albany Academy and, while there, discovered mutual electromagnetic induction (magnets) and went on become the first secretary of the Smithsonian. Henry created the first weather bureau by having military personnel send, via telegraph, daily weather reports from a number of locations around the country, and he also published what may be the first weather map.

Before the 1950s, few women were in the field, but that changed when Joanne Simpson became the first female meteorologist in 1949. Others followed, including Albany-born Maribeth Stolzenburg, whose work has helped bring the fields of atmospheric electricity and dynamical meteorology closer together.

All of these local scientists have one thing in common: the curiosity and drive to ask questions and seek answers through reason, resourcefulness and perseverance. I have been fortunate to know Cheng, Blanchard, Schaefer and Vonnegut personally. Schaefer was a mentor of mine during the '70s when I was an Albany City archaeologist and pine bush preservationist. Roger Cheng taught me how to use an electron microscope and continues to be a mentor and friend. All of these people have been an inspiration. Some of us are just lucky to be in the right place at the right time.